Participatory I

through

Investment Banks
and
Commercial Banks

Participatory Financing

through

Investment Banks

and

Commercial Banks

A.L.M. Abdul Gafoor

apptec

Participatory Financing through Investment Banks
and Commercial Banks
by
A.L.M. Abdul Gafoor

Published by
Apptec Publications
Berkenlaan 75
9741 JL Groningen
The Netherlands
Fax + Phone: (+31) 050-5775136

ISBN 90-802354-2-3

Typeset in the Netherlands
Printed in Malaysia

to

the memory of

my grandmother

Fathima

CONTENTS

*In The Name of
Allah –
Most Merciful Most
Compassionate*

Preface

Bismillahir-Rahmanir-Rahim

This is the second of a series of three books which, taken together, are expected to provide a comprehensive banking system that addresses the concerns and needs of Muslims today. Muslims are concerned that modern conventional banking system is essentially based on interest — it lends money on interest and pays interest on deposits — dealing in which is prohibited by their religion. But they cannot do without a banking system either. This problem is the subject of the first book — *Interest-free Commercial Banking* — which presents a banking system that is free of interest, and yet is fully viable and compatible with current practices in the conventional system.

In that system time and savings deposits will not bear any interest but the capital will be guaranteed. This is fine if the depositor's main aim is to keep his savings safe. But what if his primary aim is to use this capital to earn an income? Islam prohibits interest earnings. He could engage himself in some trade which Islam permits — on his own or in partnership with others, even as a sleeping partner — but it may not be possible for many for personal reasons or for reasons of the modern day environments. Exploring the possibilities of accommodating such capital holders through a bank is the subject of this book.

Studying the type and size of such capital and their owners' geographical distribution, and the type, size and distribution characteristics of investment opportunities, we present a single scheme with several options for bringing capital and entrepreneur together through banks in a mutually beneficial and responsible manner. The scheme can be offered through investment companies as well.

Inflation erodes the value of the depositor's savings as well as that of the bank's loans. This is a worrying phenomenon, especially in the developing world. The third book — *Commercial Banking in the presence of Inflation* — studies this phenomenon and presents a way of counteracting the effects of inflation. The method is applicable irrespective of whether the bank is an interest-free one or a conventional one and therefore suitable for general adoption. But it is especially relevant to Muslims for two reasons: One, since most of them live in developing countries they are most affected by it. Two, whereas in a conventional system the depositors might be fully or partially compensated by the paid interest, in an interest-free system they will have to bear the full loss. Therefore an interest-free method of compensating for that loss becomes very necessary.

I wish to thank Professor Elmer Sterken and Dr A. Tourani Rad for reading through the draft and commenting on the contents. Also to Professor Jan Oorburg and Dr Fouad Koudjeti for their comments on the manuscript, and to Yasir Diab for the final reading. All errors and shortcomings are, of course, mine. I am indebted to my family and friends for their moral support.

Groningen, the Netherlands   **A.L.M. Abdul Gafoor**
9 April 1996
(e-mail: abdul@noord.bart.nl)

274. Those who spend their wealth by night and day, by stealth and openly, verily their reward is with their Lord, and there shall no fear come upon them neither shall they grieve.

275. Those who swallow usury cannot rise up save as he ariseth whom the devil hath prostrated by (his) touch. That is because they say: Trade is like usury; whereas Allah permitteth trading and forbiddeth usury. He unto whom an admonition from his Lord cometh, and (he) refraineth (in obedience thereto), he shall keep (the profits of) that which is past, and his affair (henceforth) is with Allah. As for him who returneth (to usury) — Such are rightful owners of the Fire. They will abide therein.

276. Allah hath blighted usury and made almsgiving fruitful. Allah loveth not the impious and guilty.

277. Lo! those who believe and do good works and establish worship and pay the poor-due, their reward is with their Lord and there shall no fear come upon them neither shall they grieve.

278. O ye who believe! Observe your duty to Allah, and give up what remaineth (due to you) from usury, if ye are (in truth) believers.

279. And if ye do not, then be warned of war (against you) from Allah and His messenger. And if ye repent, then ye have your principal (without interest). Wrong not, and ye shall not be wronged.

280. And if the debtor is in straitened circum-stances, then (let there be) postponement to (the time of) ease; and that ye remit the debt as alms-giving would be better for you if ye did but know.

281. And guard yourselves against a day in which ye will be brought back to Allah. Then every soul will be paid in full that which it hath earned, and they will not be wronged.

Al-Qur'an III 130

130. O ye who believe! Devour not usury, doubling and quadrupling (the sum lent). Observe your duty to Allah that ye may be successful.

Al-Qur'an IV 161

161. And of their taking usury when they were forbidden it, and of their devouring people's wealth by false pretences. We have prepared for those of them who disbelieve a painful doom.

Al-Qur'an XXX 39

39. That which ye give in usury in order that it may increase on (other) people's property hath no increase with Allah; but that which ye give in charity, seeking Allah's countenance, hath increase manifold.

(Al-Qur'an. Translated by Marmaduke Pickthall)

HADITH

Abdullah (b. Masud) (May Allah be pleased with him) said that Allah's Messenger (May peace be upon him) cursed the one who accepted interest and the one who paid it. I asked about the one who recorded it, and the two witnesses to it. He (the narrator) said: We narrate what we have heard.

Jabir (May Allah be pleased with him) said that Allah's Messenger (May peace be upon him) cursed the acceptor of interest and its payer, and the one who records it, and the two witnesses; and he said: They are all equal.

(Sahih Muslim Hadith nos. 3880 and 3881.
Translated by Abdul Hamid Siddiqi)

Chapter 1

Introduction

C onsider a person holding his entire possession[1] in the form of cash (notes and coins) and property only. We will concern ourselves in this study only with his cash. This cash can be classed into two categories. One, that is spent on regular or immediate needs, and the other, that is not required for such use. Again, our concern is only with the latter kind of cash. A person in possession of such cash has three broad options. He can keep it safe, lend it, or invest it, depending on what he wants to achieve with it. Each of these options can be exercised in different ways.

For example, the first option can be exercised by keeping it with himself as cash, giving it to a reliable person for safekeeping, or by depositing it with a bank in a current account (demand deposit). The idea here is that the money is safe and readily available. The second option can be exercised by giving it as a loan to a known reliable person, or by depositing it with a bank in a savings account. Here the money is kept safe but it is not readily available if needed. The compensation is that the loan or the savings deposit might earn a known amount as interest. In the third option, one can a) invest in a project such as a business (his own or jointly with others) or buy a share in the stock market, or b) keep it with a bank in a time deposit account or buy a bond. In the first case, neither the capital nor the return is guaranteed. In the second, the

---

[1] That is, his own and excludes any borrowed holdings or anything held in trust.

capital and return are both guaranteed. In both, however, the common aim is to earn an income.

In Islam, these three options seem to be clearly distinguished and are governed by different rules. The first option would invoke the *zakaat*[2] rules, the second is subject to the *riba*[3] prohibition rule, and the third would be governed by the rules of commerce in case a) and by the *riba* prohibition rule in case b).

Exercising one's options through modern banks sometimes comes into conflict with the rules of Islam. This is of great concern to Muslims. Let's take them one by one.

There seems to be no problem in exercising the first option — keeping one's wealth safe — with or without the banks. The second option — lending it — has provoked the greatest interest, controversy and condemnation — both in history and in the present time. We have dealt with the second option and its exercise through modern commercial banks — the question of savings deposits and their use by the bank in advancing loans — without dealing in the prohibited *riba* in a previous publication.[4]

That leaves us with the third option: investing it. We have already seen that there are two cases in this option: invest in some project, where neither the capital nor the return is guaranteed, or invest in a bond or a fixed deposit account where the capital and return are both guaranteed. The latter, however, clearly falls under the category of *riba* which is prohibited in Islam. In this study, therefore, we

---

[2] Religious tax on wealth.
[3] Interest or usury.
[4] Gafoor (1995).

will limit ourselves to the first case under the third option, i.e. investing in a project, where neither the capital nor return is guaranteed. Again, we will confine ourselves to finding ways of effecting such an investment through a modern bank.

At this point it is useful to remind ourselves, once again, the kind of money (cash) we are concerned with in this study. It is money one owns that is not needed for consumption purposes, transaction purposes or for use in the immediate future. This is money that is to be used for bringing in an income. The size of this capital is not very relevant — it can vary from hundreds or thousands to millions.

We will first develop, in chapter 2, a general model of a financing scheme which is applicable to all projects. We will call this scheme *participatory financing*. A study of the capital-size distribution of the projects as well as that of the investors would lead us to recognise that larger size investors and larger size projects should be treated differently from their smaller counterparts. We will take a closer look at these in chapter 3, where *participatory financing* is further developed to provide it through investment banks and through commercial banks on account of their different characteristics.

Financing community projects through *participatory financing* by commercial banks is specially developed as of particular importance on account of its immediate relevance to Muslims (and others) living in developing countries.

The scheme is very promising but there are concerns too. They are dealt with in chapter 4. The scheme can be offered through investment companies as well which will enable it to become available in all countries, and almost immediately, since no government or banking authority permission need be obtained.

Up to now inflation had not entered our discussions. But inflation is a fact of life in most countries. Therefore we look at the effects of inflation on our scheme in chapter 5. Chapter 6 gives a summary and conclusion.

The mathematical relationships among the different variables are derived and presented in Appendix A. The values in tables 1 to 6 are computed using these relationships. Several conclusions are also arrived at by analysing these relationships. This and chapter 5 can be skipped on first reading. Some banking terms and processes are explained in Appendix B. Appendix C presents definitions and explanations of some terms and procedures relating to participatory financing stocks and shares. In fact it is a basic working model. The main aim however is to highlight the issues that must be addressed in developing an operational model.

Chapter 2

Participatory Financing

I slamic bankers have introduced the concepts of investment accounts and profit-and-loss-sharing into commercial banking. In practice, depositors' funds in the investment accounts are used by the Islamic banks to finance projects by entrepreneurs. The profits (or losses) are shared by the three participating parties — depositor, bank and the entrepreneur — in a pre-arranged ratio.[1] They have, however, run into serious difficulties in implementing it, mainly because it is applied to situations where it is inappropriate. We have dealt with it elsewhere.[2] Here we take these basic concepts and, combining them with the credit-creating ability of commercial banks, devise a financing scheme that is both transparent in concept and easy to implement.

2.1 The basic concepts

2.1.1 Profit and loss sharing

The concept of profit-and-loss-sharing is based on the old Meccan practice of *Mudaraba*[3] which has been adopted by Islam. In the main form of *mudaraba* there are two partners: the entrepreneur and the financier. The entrepreneur has the knowledge and necessary skills to

---

[1] See, for example, Ahmad (1981), Iqbal and Mirakhor (1987), Siddiqi (1988), Rad (1991), IPS (1994), etc.
[2] Gafoor (1995). See also Rad (1991), Qadir (1994), Zaman (1994), Ahmad (1994) etc.
[3] See Saleh (1986) for a very good explanation of *mudaraba*, pp.101-114.

undertake an enterprise and the financier has the funds. The entrepreneur has full control of the enterprise; the financier provides only the funds. The net profit of the enterprise is shared by the two parties equally or in a pre-arranged fashion. When there is a loss, however, the total loss is borne only by the financier. (Strictly speaking, then, this is not a fully profit-*and*-loss-sharing partnership but a profit-sharing-and-loss-absorbing partnership. For this reason, let us call it by its original name — *mudaraba* partnership.)   We need not go into other details or variations of this main form such as the financier also taking part in the management or other activities of the enterprise or the entrepreneur also providing a portion of the funds.

When the bank entered the picture, the financier became the investor and the Islamic bankers divided this threesome into two twosomes: investor and the bank on the one hand and the bank and the entrepreneur on the other. In the first case the bank is the entrepreneur and in the second case the bank is the financier. The division of profit and loss was done accordingly on a pre-arranged fashion.

2.1.2 Investment accounts

Investment accounts in a commercial bank is an invention of the Islamic banks. These are time deposit accounts accepted by the bank on the explicit understanding that the funds will be invested in projects on a "profit-and-loss-sharing" basis. These accounts bear no interest, and there is no guarantee of capital, nor of profit. It is a partnership sharing all risks. In the following discussions it will be a full *mudaraba* partnership as defined above.

2.1.3 Credit creation and bank money

Commercial banks can create credit. This is their special privilege. It means that they can lend more money than they actually have in their possession. How much more they can lend depends on their assumption, based on their experience, about how much money, in cash, will be demanded by their depositors, on the average, at any given time. If they assume that they can meet all their cash demands by, say, 10 percent of the cash in their possession, then it is pointless, from their point of view, holding the rest of the 90 percent of the cash in their hands. They would rather lend it to their customers and earn interest. This 10 percent is called cash reserve ratio. The smaller this ratio the more they can lend and make an earning in the form of interest.

This, however, is entirely dependent on the behaviour of the deposit holding public and their trust and confidence in their bank that their money is safe with the bank and that it will be returned to them on demand or as previously agreed. Should any bank fail to honour this trust at any time, it could lead to a run on — *i.e.* a rush to withdraw deposits from — all the banks and disaster to the entire banking system. In order to prevent such an eventuality and to keep the confidence of the public in the ability of the banks to meet their cash demands on their deposits, and for other reasons such as controlling the money supply, the Central Bank is authorised to monitor and control and change as necessary this cash reserve ratio.[4]

Suppose a customer deposits $1000 in cash into his account. Assuming that the cash reserve ratio is 10 percent, the bank can advance up to $9000 in loans on the

---

[4] See any textbook on banking.

strength of this cash deposit. This is credit creation.[5] The $9000, which does not exist in reality but only in the books of the bank, is called bank money. Yet, for all intentions and purposes it is money as good as any.[6]

Thus, this credit creating mechanism allows a commercial bank to grant advances and loans and thereby finance projects several times more worth than any individual or any other entity can finance with the same amount of money. Consequently, it reaps a huge amount of profit in terms of interest from a small amount of real cash, which itself is not its own! This is a special privilege of a commercial bank.

2.1.4 Financing with bank money

We propose to use this bank money to finance projects on a full *mudaraba* partnership basis, instead of lending it on interest. In order to explain the concept, let us take an example.

Continuing the same example from the previous section, suppose a customer opens an investment account depositing $1000 in cash. Assuming that the cash reserve ratio is 10 percent, the bank can advance up to $9000 to finance a project. If the bank becomes a partner in an enterprise it will go into partnership with this amount as its capital investment. When a profit is declared by the joint enterprise it will be computed on the basis of $9000 as capital investment. But the real cash involved was only $1000; the $9000 was created by the bank. Suppose the

---

[5] For an explanation of the mechanism of credit creation by commercial banks, see, for example, Robertson (1937), Korteweg and Keesing (1959), King (1987), Siddiqi (1988) etc. See also the footnote in Appendix A.

[6] Withers (1923). See Appendix B.

enterprise's profit was $10 per $1000, which is one percent, then the total profit would be $90. However the actual money involved was only $1000 and thus the bank gets $90 per $1000. That is, the bank in reality earns a nine percent profit. Thus though the declared profit was only one percent — a very low yield — the real profit was nine percent which is undoubtedly a very good profit. This is because the project was financed by bank money, thanks to the participation of a commercial bank in the project.

To drive the point home, let us assume that a private individual invested $9000 of his own money and the bank invested $9000. Capitals being equal, they will have equal share in the profit (not considering the labour/management input on either side). In our example, $90 for the bank and $90 for the individual. The individual's profit is $90 for $9000 and hence a rate of return of one percent. But the bank's rate of return is really nine percent, because the $9000 used by the bank was bank money created on the strength of $1000 in the investment account.

It is this mechanism that we propose to exploit in financing commercial and social projects in a way that equitably rewards the participants in the project: the investor, the bank and the entrepreneur. This would enable the commercial banks to contribute to national development in a uniquely meaningful manner and with responsibility.

2.2 The general mechanism

The basic concepts of *mudaraba* partnership, investment accounts and credit creation have been explained in the previous section. Using these we developed the concept of financing with bank money. In this section we will develop a mechanism of investing funds from the investment accounts, managing their investment, and sharing the profits and losses therefrom. We will call this *participatory financing*.

2.2.1 The partners and their shares

In the proposed scheme of Participatory Financing, there are three partners: the investor, the bank and the entrepreneur. The investor is a pure financier, he invests his money and plays no further part in the project. The entrepreneur is a pure entrepreneur, he is fully in-charge of the project and invests no money in his capacity as an entrepreneur. The bank, however, is in a peculiar position: it is both an investor — though investing other peoples' money and "multiplying" it — and an entrepreneur to the extent of identifying viable projects and ensuring their proper accounting and management. The bank invests neither its own money nor its own ideas, yet it provides a very useful intermediary and trustee part and takes responsibility. The proposed mechanism will reward the bank for this useful role it plays but will punish if it fails.

With the above in mind, we propose an equal share to all three partners when there is a profit. When a loss occurs, the entrepreneur will bear no part of it, but the bank and the investor will share the loss equally between themselves.[7]

To clarify, continuing our example of section 2.1.4, where the bank invested $9000 and the profit was $90 (i.e. a one

---

[7] This is our suggestion, and the figures make the arithmetic simple which makes it easy to explain the principles involved. In practice, however, the banks are naturally free to set their own ratios or negotiate with their partners.

percent profit), the entrepreneur will receive $30 (i.e. one-third of the profit), the bank $30 and the investor $30. The investor's actual deposit was $1000. Hence he receives a three percent return on his investment.

Suppose in the above scenario, the project suffered a one percent loss, i.e. a loss of $90. The total loss will be borne by the financiers: the bank and the investor. Sharing the loss equally between the bank and the investor, the bank will lose $45 and the investor $45. This is a 4.5 percent loss to the investor. The bank did not invest any money of its own, yet in the event of a loss it will have to bear its share. The real financier is the investor, but the bank is the trustee and the "money-multiplier". It is the responsibility it takes to identify viable projects and to ensure their proper accounting and management that entitles it to a share in the profit. On the other hand it is the possibility of a loss that should make it vigilant in its responsibility.

When there is no loss or profit none of the partners suffer any loss or receive any profit.

In Table 1 given below we present these three and two other scenarios so that the profit/loss distribution scheme could be fully understood. The first three scenarios of the table represent what has been explained above. The last two scenarios show how greatly the profits are multiplied when the profit is higher. For example, when the profit is 10 per cent, the investor gets a 30 percent return; and nearly half his investment when the project's profit rises by just another 5 percent. The bank and the entrepreneur get the same profits but theirs cannot be given in terms of return on investment since they began with no investment of their own. Their profit is for successfully "handling" a project of that size.

We see clearly, that so long as there is no loss everybody stands to gain, however small the profit may be. And the gain increases many fold as the project makes higher profits. When there is a loss, however, both the investor and the bank lose heavily while the entrepreneur is unaffected.

Table 1. Profit/loss distribution among the partners
(Investment: $1000 cash, providing $9000 in bank money)

Scenario	Project		Investor		Bank	Entrepreneur
	Amount	%	Amount	%	Amount	Amount
1.	90	1	30	3	30	30
2.	0	0	0	0	0	0
3.	-90	-1	-45	-4.5	-45	0
4.	900	10	300	30	300	300
5.	1350	15	450	45	450	450
Share in:						
profit	1		1/3		1/3	1/3
loss	1		1/2		1/2	0

2.2.2 A pool of funds and a series of projects

So far in our discussion, we had one project which had a definite beginning and end, such as a trade caravan in the old days. The financing could have been by one person or more but that made no difference to the argument. In the present context, however, instead of the direct financier-entrepreneur contract of old, we now have an intermediary

— the bank. Consequently we have two contracts: one where the bank and the entrepreneur are the parties and the other where the bank and the investor are the parties. In addition, the bank has to deal with several entrepreneurs (and projects) and several investors simultaneously; and for long periods of time or indefinitely. Therefore, though we can adopt the concepts and principles of *mudaraba* partnerships of old, new operational procedures have to be developed taking into account current situations. We will develop an outline of such procedures in the following paragraphs.

First of all, these projects begin at different times and, some may end after some time and others may continue indefinitely. Secondly, it is obvious that we cannot establish a direct link between any one investor and any one project; neither a one-to-many nor a many-to-one direct relationship. The situation is that we have a number of projects running simultaneously and a pool of money from several investors which finances the projects. To accommodate these two situations we have to make some changes to the old practices.

As far as the first contract — that of the bank and the entrepreneur — is concerned, there is a direct connection between the parties; and the concerned project and its duration (or the dates of commencement and termination) are well defined. This is necessary in order to determine the profit/loss of the project and to share it between the parties. If the duration of the project is less than one year, the *mudaraba* contract is well defined and there is no problem. If the project runs beyond one year, profit/loss may have to be computed and shared annually.[8]

In the second contract — that of the investor and the bank — there is no problem as to the direct link between the parties. The duration of this contract too is well defined — it lasts as long as the money is kept with the bank. But this contract does not relate to any given project, and thus to no particular profit or loss. So a practical solution has to be found to make the connection in this three-way partnership in order to compute and share the profit/loss.

Assuming that profit and loss accounting is done annually, it looks a more practical solution to consider the *total* net profit/loss of the bank from *all* projects *together* for *each accounting year* and share the profit/loss between the bank and the investors *annually*. Consequently, from the investor's point of view, all of the bank's Participatory Financing operations could be considered as one single project of one year duration.

One of the advantages in treating all the projects together is that a loss in one project may be covered by gains in the other projects. This is very important.

2.2.3 Stocks and shares

Now, there is the related problem of deciding when an investment became entitled to a share in the profit/loss — from the first day of deposit or later? There are two cases. One, the investor's share begins with the first day of deposit and ends the day he withdraws it. This is quite acceptable when the system is fully up and running. If someone invested on 1 January and withdrew on

---

[8] Actually the accounting period, which can be a quarter or half-a-year.

31 December, then he will receive his full share of profit/loss for the year according to the size of his investment. In case he kept his money for four months, say, from 1 August to 30 November he will get one-third the full share.

The second case is when the system is still in its formative stages. Here there is a lead period before projects are identified, evaluated and capital granted. And there is the gestation period of the project itself. So there is a period, from one to several years, where there is no yield at all on the investment. If an investor withdrew at this stage he will possibly sustain a loss. What would be even more unfair is that should another one come in at this point, he immediately starts off with a claim to profit, which his predecessor would have been entitled to had he stayed on.

The above two cases point to the existence of two types of investment in Participatory Financing (PF). The former is more like stocks[9] and the latter is like shares. In this case our original investor of the previous example would have been able to sell his shares to the second investor and thus receive some benefit for the period when his investment was not earning any profit.

Thus we can talk about Participatory Financing Stocks and Participatory Financing Shares. The difference between normal stocks and PF stocks would be that: 1) PF stocks will not bear any fixed rate of return or interest, 2) PF stocks are not transferable because there is no advantage, 3) PF stocks have no priority claims over PF shares, 4) PF stocks too share in profit and loss. On the other hand, PF shares are precisely the same as normal shares: 1) PF

---

[9] As understood in the UK.

shares earn no profit or loss in the first few years, say one to three years. 2) PF shares are transferable and therefore have no termination points. But PF shares will have a stake in the assets of the projects whereas the PF stocks will not have any such claim. However, since the investors have no direct connection with any particular project, the claims of the PF shares are on all of the Bank's PF operations. Thus, if, for example, a project ends and the assets are sold off or the bank sells off its shares in a project (perhaps to the entrepreneur or to an outside investor) the proceeds from such sales will accrue to all the PF shares (providing interim dividends, additional PF shares or increasing their value).

Whether the stocks and shares are issued periodically, as and when necessary or are available throughout the year; whether they are for fixed terms or not, are all operational concerns and are matters for individual bank's decision. So is the decision as to whether the stocks and shares have different profit ratios or the same. The bank may also consider issuing separate stocks and shares to different groups of projects, instead of all the investors having claims to all the projects of the bank.

In Appendix C we present some working definitions of terms and procedures which can be used as a basis for the development of an operational model. The main purpose here is to indicate the many issues that should be addressed in devising such a model.

2.2.5 Accounts and management

In the system described above the bank is a full partner in all the projects it finances. Consequently it has the right of access to all the books of the enterprise. It may have no say in the running of the enterprise as such — this is the exclusive domain of the entrepreneur, and the bank is not expected to have any expertise in the matter — but the accounts of the project are available to the bank at all times and it may step in if any financial mismanagement or false accounting is discovered. This is to safeguard the interests of both the investors and the bank, because if there is any loss both will suffer the consequences and the bank is accountable to both the investors and its own share holders.

2.3 Application

The concepts and mechanism developed in the previous sections are universally applicable to all situations. However, there are a great many variations in the situations — with respect to the entrepreneurs, banks and the investors as well as with respect to the projects (its size, duration, profitability and risk) and the environment in which these investment operations take place. The spectrum may extend from big banks financing large projects with high profit expectations using funds from few very heavy investors to small banks financing low profit projects using funds from a large number of small investors. Projects themselves may be of short or long duration, they may have high or low risk, may be only economically or socially relevant or a mixture of both, they may be located in urban areas or rural areas, of industrial or agricultural in nature, or national or local in scope.

Each bank may find itself at one or more points in this multi-faceted spectrum of different situations. It is necessary that the bank carefully assesses its own situation(s) and tailors its participatory financing scheme accordingly, if the scheme is to work successfully. We will not go into the details in this short essay.

2.4 Some caution

One of the objections raised against Islamic banks when they apply for commercial banking permission in countries where the conventional system of banking exists is that, most of their assets being tied up in investments without any guarantee as to the capital or the return, it is difficult to put a value to their assets. According to a financial advisor:[10]

> The Bank of England, under the 1979 Act, would have great difficulty in putting a value on the assets of an Islamic institution which wanted to operate as a bank in the UK. The traditional banking system has much of its assets in fixed interest instruments and it is comparatively easy to value that. For example, if they are British Government instruments they will have a quoted market value; and there are recognised methods for valuing traditional banking assets when they become non-productive. But it is very difficult indeed to value an Islamic asset such as a share in a joint venture; and the Bank of England would have to send a team of experienced accountants into every Islamic bank operating in the UK as a bank under the 1979 Act, to try to put a proper and cautious value on its assets.

This is a valid concern and the problem still exists under the proposed participatory financing scheme. Methods have to be found to overcome this problem whether the bank is operating under conventional environment or otherwise. But more so in the former.

---

[10] Steele (1984)

The problem is not in the creation of bank money but in its use. The loans advanced by conventional commercial banks are the same bank created money. But these loans have a fixed return and the capital is fully recoverable — at least in theory. The problem with putting that same money into investment is that both the above certainties are absent. This can affect both the bank's solvency as well as its liquidity; and both have consequences for the entire banking system. It is for this reason that conventional commercial banks are prohibited from engaging in investment activities on their own. Even when permitted it is restricted to Government securities only. For, they are readily marketable and the capital is largely secure; only the return is variable, yet its going market rate is readily assessable.

One possible safeguard is to increase the reserve ratio for the investment accounts (to 100 percent?) and/or to require an increase in the bank's share capital proportionate to its investment holdings in order to cover possible losses.

2.4.1 Options

The first option will make the bank essentially an investment bank and we will loose the advantage we seek to exploit using the commercial bank's ability to create credit. The second option will limit the amount of money the bank can accept into its investment accounts due to its own capital limitation.

Both these options are, however, neither contradictory nor do they lessen the value of our proposed participatory financing scheme. Because they, in fact, cater to two different categories of investors and therefore are complementary.

It is a fact of life, in all societies, that the distribution of wealth follows a very skewed pattern — a large proportion of the society's wealth is concentrated in the hands of a small fraction of the population. Consequently, we have two categories of investors: one group with large amounts of money to invest and another, much larger, with much smaller amounts.

In the next chapter we will see how these two groups of investors can be matched with the two options we saw earlier and how the participatory financing scheme can be utilised in both cases.

Chapter 3

Two Groups and Two Options

We ended the last chapter with the identification of two broad categories of investors and two banking options to cater to their needs. In this chapter we will see how these two groups of investors can be matched with the two options and how the participatory financing scheme can be utilised in both cases. The first problem one will face here is defining the two groups in practical terms. That is, who is a large investor and who is small. This is necessarily relative. It depends on the size and wealth of the country concerned as well as on the size and share capital of the bank concerned. Broadly speaking, we may consider a small number of wealthy individuals and many institutional investors as falling into the first category and the majority of the time and savings account holders as falling into the second. Here we will leave it at that and concern ourselves only with the concepts involved.

3.1 Large investors and investment banks

Commercial banks are normally not permitted to engage in private sector investment activities. Even if they were to be permitted under special circumstances, as we saw earlier, their capital position will exclude them from engaging in large scale activities. This leaves the large investor with three options: to invest in his own project and enjoy the profit/loss entirely by himself, go into partnership with others (including buying a share in a company) and share the profit/loss, or open an account with an investment bank. We leave out the first two options as not concerning us here in this study. Then if we consider only the third — bank option — and stay with the *riba* prohibition and *mudaraba* partnership, we come to the participatory financing we saw in the second chapter — minus the bank-money part.

It means then that the investors with large amounts of money will seek *investment banks* who *participate-finance* projects. These investors are people who have money with which they wish to earn an income. They are prohibited by their religion to earn an income by lending their money and are encouraged by the same religion to employ their wealth in productive enterprise. Or they are people convinced of the evil of lending on interest, yet in need of earning an income using their capital. It is necessary that these people be provided with a means that will cater to their needs, keeping in mind their constraints.

The originators of Islamic banking had this in mind when they formulated their concepts, but by mixing it up with commercial banking fell short of their aim.[1] Commercial banks serve purposes different from those of investment banks. They perform different functions, employ different methods and procedures, and cater to different groups of clientele. Therefore we propose that Islamic investment banks, which operate on the basis of participatory financing, be established as *separate* entities — separate from Islamic commercial banks which provide all commercial banking services but without involving in *riba*.[2]

---

[1] See Gafoor (1995), pp.44-71.

[2] It is possible for Islamic commercial banks to be involved in investment activities, indeed very usefully and meaningfully — but as an *option* and under different circumstances and conditions. We will explore these in the next sections.

Now, when such a differentiation is made some adjustments have to be made to the participatory financing scheme we developed in the previous chapter. Since investment banks cannot create credit, the money multiplier function is absent, and consequently the profits are going to be not as high as when commercial banks participate-finance. The bank's role is now reduced to identifying viable projects and to ensuring their proper accounting and management, besides collection of funds and disbursement of dividends. As such, perhaps, their share in the profit/loss may now be set a little low. For example, the profit/loss proportion between the investor and the bank may now be set at 2:1, instead of the earlier 1:1 ratio. As earlier, the entrepreneur will have one-third in the profits and no part in the loss. In this case our earlier Table 1 will take the form in Table 2. Note that here instead of $1000 cash being multiplied into $9000 bank money, it is now $9000 cash directly from the investor.

Comparing tables 1 and 2 we see that the entrepreneur gets the same benefit for "handling" a project of the same size, irrespective of the source of its funding — commercial bank or investment bank. The money being bank-created or not does not make any difference to the return he receives for the services he provides. The bank's returns (both profit and loss) are reduced. This is on account of its reduced involvement — investment banks do not create credit. It is the investor whose profit/loss are much more tempered. His profit rate is much reduced — from 3 to 0.444 percent in scenarios 1 (in tables 1 and 2); and from 30 and 45 to 4.444 and 6.666 respectively in scenarios 4 and 5. But the rate of his loss is also reduced — from -4.5 to -0.666 (scenarios 3).

The main consequence of these results is that the investors depositing with investment banks would require the bank to go for high-yield projects. Investment banks would therefore try to avoid low-yield projects and concentrate on high-yield ones.

Table 2. Profit/loss distribution among the partners
(Investment: $9000 cash)

Scen-ario	Project		Investor		Bank	Entre-preneur
	Amount	%	Amount	%	Amount	Amount
1.	90	1	40	0.444	20	30
2.	0	0	0	0	0	0
3.	-90	-1	-60	-0.666	-30	0
4.	900	10	400	4.444	200	300
5.	1350	15	600	6.666	300	450
Share in:						
profit	1		4/9		2/9	3/9
loss	1		2/3		1/3	0

3.2 Small investors and commercial banks

There are two reasons for people to hold some of their wealth in time or savings accounts. One is safekeeping and the other is to earn an income through interest. The latter is prohibited in Islam. In order to provide an alternative income Islamic banks offered to provide them a share in the profit made in their *mudaraba/musharaka*[3] operations using funds from these accounts. But this contradicted with the first reason — safety of capital — because if there was a loss that too should be shared by the account holders. The resulting complications have been considered in detail in an earlier study: Since interest from time and savings accounts is prohibited to Muslims their purpose in keeping such accounts can only be the safety of their capital. Consequently funds from these accounts cannot be used in *mudaraba/musharaka* type operations. Therefore it was suggested that these funds be used only to grant loans free of interest but with a service charge.[4] This would guarantee the safety of the deposit and, at the same time, reward the bank for the services it provides. A theoretical foundation has been provided using a simple model of the commercial bank lending operation.[5]

---

[3] Musharaka is a temporary equity participation agreement between a bank and clients for effecting a certain operation within an agreed period of time. Both parties contribute to the capital of the operation in varying degrees and agree to divide the net profits or losses in proportions agreed upon in advance. Iqbal and Mirakhor (1987), p.59.

[4] Gafoor (1995), pp.66-71.

[5] This model calls the "interest" charged by conventional banks as the cost of borrowing and it is considered as consisting of six components: interest, services cost, overheads cost, a risk premium, compensation for inflation and bank's profit. The first component is the amount paid to the depositor as interest whose money the bank lends to the borrowers. This is pure *riba*. It is shown that the other five components do not include any form of *riba*. Hence if the first component — the only one which is *riba* — is removed from both sides, the resulting cost of borrowing, which is the amount the borrower pays the bank for the services he receives, is free of *riba*. Such removal is possible because if the depositors do not demand an interest on their deposits, the bank need not collect it from the borrowers to be passed onto the depositors. *ibid.* pp.3-20.

To those Muslims whose primary aim in holding their wealth in time or savings accounts is safety, this suggestion serves well. Then, what about those whose primary aim is to earn an income using their wealth? First, what are their characteristics? They are large in number, scattered all over the country, and most of them hold small amounts to their credit. It is this group of investors that are our concern in this section.

To this group too Islam offers only one option: use it in a productive enterprise (such as trade), take all the risks involved and enjoy the fruits — profit or loss. If they are to use a bank for this purpose, the only option is to put the money in a m*udaraba*-based (i.e. profit and loss sharing) investment account — whether that bank is an investment bank or a commercial bank.

Commercial banks have some advantages which investment banks hardly enjoy. Investment banks generally have minimum amount requirements to open an account with them and these minimum amounts are often much higher than the balances held by the majority of those who hold time or savings accounts with commercial banks. For reasons we saw in the previous section, they will also tend to finance only large high-yield projects. Added to these, they are primarily located in capital cities and other very large cities, while commercial banks reach out to small towns and other population centres. Thus the commercial banks both cater to, and are in close proximity to, small investors *and* small entrepreneurs. This makes them ideal intermediaries to bring these two groups of people together for mutual benefit. Combined with their ability to create credit, they can be a powerful tool in bringing about private enterprise economic development at the local level.

Considering the fact that the credits advanced to financed enterprises will primarily circulate in the locality and within the local banks and that the total funds available in the investment accounts of such local banks would be comparatively small, both the liquidity and solvency concerns could be fairly easily managed using either or both the reserve ratio and proportionate share capital requirements.

Many of the economic and social problems as well as the large scale rural-to-urban migration can be traced to the lack of economic activity at the local level resulting in large scale unemployment. Bringing together local capital and local talent and entrepreneurship to engage in local projects could greatly help towards alleviating these problems.

Local level economic activities too can be divided into two groups. One, the normal small and medium scale private enterprises — commercial, industrial, agricultural and others — where the profit expectations are high or at least reasonable. Two, similar private enterprises but which are to be located in rural areas and in the poor sections of large towns and cities. Here the expected turnovers and margins will be low since such communities could not afford the going market prices. This is the reason why normal business entrepreneurs would keep out of these areas. But when commercial banks participate-finance such enterprises they will become viable on account of the money-multiplier factor. Yet the prime motive in these enterprises will be community development. We will consider them below separately.

3.2.1 Private enterprises

This is the traditional area of commercial bank lending activity. Businesses and individuals borrow money from the bank for various activities including short-term loans and advances to manage cash flow requirements, and medium- and long-term loans to expand current activities and to establish new enterprises. The last is very suitable for participate financing, while the former two are not so amenable. The reasons have been extensively discussed elsewhere.[6] This distinction between the two types of uses which borrowed money is put to, and which was not important when money was lent on interest and therefore perhaps not even recognised, becomes very important when financing is done on the basis of profit and loss sharing. The failure to recognise this seems to be the main reason for the problems faced by the Islamic banks. It has been suggested there that the former types of uses be met by lending money with a service charge.[7] Here we will consider the last type of use.

Perhaps it should be mentioned at this point that participatory financing is not necessary for the existence and successful operation of an interest-free commercial bank. Such a bank — accepting deposits on its current, time and savings accounts without paying any interest but guaranteeing capital, and lending money levying service charges — can function independently of any participatory financing activity. The size of such a bank, however, will be limited by the amount of money deposited by clients whose primary aim is the safety of their capital and its ready availability when needed. The participatory financing we will consider in this section and in the next is an *option* available to those commercial banks which are willing to take the risks involved, acquire the expertise and

---

[6] *ibid.* pp.42-60.
[7] *ibid.* pp.22-30 and 64-71.

skills necessary, abide by the reserve ratio and share capital regulations, and to maintain the necessary infra structures. In return they will be able to attract and/or retain the deposits of the clients whose main aim is to earn a *riba*-free income using their capital, and to earn a *riba*-free income for themselves.

The financing we are talking about here is essentially venture capital which will primarily benefit new enterprises. The bank is a full partner in the enterprise and thus has full access to all its accounts at all times. Thus many of the problems the Islamic banks presently encounter in assessing their share of the profit/loss when they lend money on PLS basis will not arise. Management of the enterprise, however, is the sole responsibility of the entrepreneur and the bank has nothing to do with it, except, perhaps, in extreme situations. Thus the bank need not have any specific expertise in any of the enterprises it finances. This too is one of the problems faced by the Islamic banks in their present schemes of financing.

The bank may continue to be a partner in the enterprise and earn an income or sell it off as a going concern when it is fully established. The latter will release funds for financing new projects. The decision is entirely up to the bank.

If the projects participate-financed by the bank are running well, the returns on the stocks and shares of the bank will be good, and more people will deposit money in the bank's investment accounts. When confidence in the bank's ability to earn positive returns grows, some of the money in the time and savings deposit accounts too might be diverted to the investment account. This will increase funds available to establish new enterprises, but will dry up funds for lending to running concerns and others.

When this happens some of the running businesses and small enterprises may have to think of joining in participatory financing schemes, making their accounts open to the bank. On the other hand, when confidence is less strong people might wish to hold their money in time and savings accounts, preferring the safety of their capital over uncertain income. There will be a constantly dynamic balance and in the long term an equilibrium may emerge.

In both cases, however, money will be available to businesses and enterprises either in the form of loans or in the form of participatory financing funds. The size of this total capital depends on the banking habits of the people concerned. This in turn depends on their knowledge and trust of, and access to, the banking system. These, in their turn, depend on the level of education and economic development of the general population.

3.2.2 Financing community projects

All the writers on Islamic banking have advocated setting aside a portion of the bank's funds for "social" lending without any charges, and sometimes even writing them off when the recipient is unable to repay. While we do not intend to recommend charity on the part of a business entity handling other people's money, we do recognise the need for financing "social" projects. These are of particular importance to the third world countries where most of the Muslims find themselves. Since no cost-free money should be expected from the investment accounts of a commercial bank, we will explore ways of meeting both objectives.

The projects we have in mind are the ones that cater to the "basic" needs of the population in the rural areas and in the poorer sections of large towns and cities. Providing these needs will contribute to the local economy, create jobs in the locality and improve living conditions. In short development at the micro level. These are the ones that lie between the non-profit making public services and enterprises, and the private enterprises with high profit expectations. This is the area where the government has neither the imagination to identify them nor the machinery to successfully implement them. Private entrepreneurs avoid them on account of their low expected turnovers and returns; their often distant location away from centres of business activity also plays apart. But these are, however, the very areas which determine the level of economic and social welfare of the population. All political parties promise them but no government delivers them. This then becomes the domain of the entrepreneur — both individuals and organisations — with the public spirit *and* no money.

If the talent and energy of such entrepreneurs can be coupled with the capital of the local investors through commercial banks, then a major step would have been taken in the direction of national development. The fact that the local banks are well aware of them and can conveniently assess and supervise them will be an added advantage. In addition, the local investors will have the satisfaction of seeing their money in useful action, perhaps even benefiting by it directly.

Examples of such projects are: farm and industrial equipment repairs and hires, local transport and communication, handicraft and cottage industries, marketing facilities for local produce, local shopping complex or market, low cost housing for the low and lower-middle classes, medical services including laboratory services, adult education and job training centres, etc. etc. The list is varied and endless, and depends on the particular situation of the local community concerned as well as on the imagination of the community leaders and entrepreneurs, and the skills and resources available locally.

The common characteristics of these projects are that they are necessary for the economic and/or social development and well-being of the community, but the expected return on them is low, may take too long to bear fruit, and the local entrepreneurs willing to embark on such projects do not have the finances and even lack the necessary collateral to seek financing from the banks. The proposed participatory financing scheme fits the bill well because the project itself becomes the collateral, the low return is augmented by the bank's money multiplier factor, and the long duration becomes less of a concern if the project has less risk and the return is constant. But the last two factors will, in addition, be mitigated by the bank also investing in other projects of lesser duration and higher profit.

The proportion of investment account funds that will be earmarked for community projects such as considered in this section and other private enterprise projects considered in the last section may be determined by the banks themselves. Alternatively, the Central Bank of the country may be given authority to determine the ratio in keeping with national/regional development needs and priorities.

Chapter 4

Promises and Concerns

The participatory financing scheme presented in the previous chapters offers great promises. But there are also concerns about its application in real life. Its promise lies first of all in providing a *halaal* way of earning an income using one's capital without having to take an active part in an enterprise. Secondly, but equally importantly, it provides the entrepreneur access to required capital without having to deal in *riba*, even in the absence of interest-free banks. In addition, this access to capital is made available without having to provide an acceptable collateral. These are very important considerations. For there are many talented and skilled persons with experience whose initiative is frustrated because of their inability to obtain capital — either on account of their refusal to approach a bank for fear of dealing in *riba* or because they have no collateral. In the event it is the community as a whole that loses the fruits of their talent. The participatory financing scheme, whether offered through investment banks or commercial banks, seems to offer an excellent promise in preventing this situation.

We have so far limited our participatory financing scheme to be implemented through banks only. There are situations where this may not be possible. And even where possible, it may prove to be insufficient or unable to cater to all the demand. The first is when the banking authorities in a country refuse to permit banks to get directly involved in such uncertain forms of investment. Some countries are reluctant to permit even investment banks to offer such schemes because of the fear that the failure of any institution with the word 'bank' in its name might bring about bad reputation to all banks and endanger the entire financial system of the country. This is a very reasonable concern. The second is that the investment banks, as we said before, may tend to limit their operations to large projects, and locate themselves only in large cities. This leaves the outlying cities, smaller communities and smaller projects entirely to the commercial banks. The latter may not be able to or willing to provide participatory financing or the demand might exceed supply. In either case, could the participatory financing scheme be offered through intermediaries other than banks — as a substitute or as complementary? We will consider this in the next section.

In a later section we will study the project size and its implication. It appears that as the project size diminishes, it will become increasingly difficult to meet the costs of the intermediary. When the limit is reached, is it time to revert to pure *mudaraba* partnership? We will look at this too. The possibility of offering the PF scheme through intermediaries other than banks seems to open great vistas. But what is the down side?

Returning to the commercial banks, assuming that they are allowed to offer PF schemes as an option, what are the implications? The promises are more enchanting and the concerns more acute when participatory financing is effected through commercial banks. There is promise that this will give additional impetus to local economic development. The primary concern is that this new form of financing by a commercial bank requires an altogether different approach to financing. Specifically, the officers entrusted with its implementation will have to have a very good understanding of the scheme, commitment to its success and, even more importantly, a good understanding of the environment in which they operate — investment needs and opportunities in the area, the business climate and the people. In short, besides being good and prudent bankers they will have to be also entrepreneurs themselves. We will address these issues briefly in sections 4.2 to 4.4.

4.1 Intermediaries other than banks

The central feature of traditional banking is capital certainty for depositors. In participatory financing there is no guarantee of capital for the investor — whether it is provided through investment banks or commercial banks. Banks which wish to offer participatory financing will face difficulties on this account when they apply for permission to the banking authorities of the country.

Referring to Islamic banking in the context of PLS[1] schemes, Sir Leigh Pemberton, the Governor of the Bank of England, told the Arab Banker's Association in London that:[2]

- A central feature of the banking system of the United Kingdom as enshrined in the legal framework is capital certainty for depositors. It is the most important feature which distinguished the banking sector from the other segments of the financial system;

- The Bank of England is not legally able to authorise under the Banking Act, an institution

---

[1] Profit-and-loss-sharing
[2] Pemberton (1984).

which does not take deposits as defined under that Act.

Mr Charles Schotta, the US Treasury Department specialist in regulatory issues has remarked that:[3]

> Any institution that wishes to use the word 'bank' in its title has to guarantee at least a zero rate of interest.

Any relaxation of this position is precluded because should a bank offering participatory financing fail, for any reason at all, it would undermine the confidence in the whole financial system, with which it is inevitably identified. As Suratgar puts it:[4]

> There could be potential dangers for the international system, where the failure of such an institution could bring with it the failure of other associated institutions, or of all the Western banking institutions which come closely tied to with such an operation.

The position will be the same in all countries which operate under the traditional system of banking. The exception will be the few Muslim countries which have allowed Islamic banks, which work under the PLS scheme, to operate. The question is: Is participatory financing doomed outside of these few countries? The answer, happily, seems to be No, since what appears to be objectionable is for such an institution to use the word 'bank' in its title and not the mode of financing. For, according to Sir Leigh:[5]

---

[3] Schotta (1985).
[4] Suratgar (1984).
[5] Pemberton (1984).

- Islamic banking is a perfectly acceptable mode of financing but it does not fall within the definition of what constitutes banking in the UK; and

- The Islamic facilities might be provided within other areas of the financial system without using a banking name.

This brings us to the possibility of offering participatory financing through institutions other than banks. Such institutions, let us call them Investment Companies, can offer the participatory financing scheme we have developed for investment banks.

4.1.1 Investment companies

The countries that allow Islamic banks to operate should have no objection to permitting participatory financing to be offered through investment banks. And, it appears from the above, that other countries too may not have any objection if it is offered through investment companies. Thus participatory financing as we have developed for investment banks can be practised in all countries. This is good news for all Muslims (and to others too, for participatory financing is a responsible form of financing). This is especially so for those living and/or investing in countries that do not permit Islamic banking, which are by far the majority.

Is all well? There is concern too. For, now that the control and supervision by the banking authorities is absent, the responsibility of operating a clean system and thereby winning the confidence and the funds of the investors falls squarely on the shoulders of the investment companies. They, of course will have to operate under the relevant company laws, but winning the confidence of the public is another matter. Their operations will have to be transparent and subject to audit. The investment companies, in turn, will have to make sure that the projects they finance are viable and the accounting is true and accurate and the financial management is sound. Establishing these companies as public limited liability companies may help in these respects.

The competence and the integrity of the entrepreneur is of crucial importance. It is on the strength of the trust in the competence and the integrity of the entrepreneur that his project was financed and its success, and even more importantly, the very future of the participatory financing scheme itself, depends on the continued existence of this trust. It is important to remember that the failure of a single entrepreneur to live up to a high level of honesty in his transactions can be bad news for the whole scheme.

The investment companies we discussed above were conceived as alternatives to investment banks. In the process we have overcome the barrier of the banking authorities and thus have made participatory financing available in all countries. They can even operate across national boundaries. Good. However, these companies are expected to cater to large investors and large projects. We have also seen that they are likely to operate from large cities. Could we not make it available to smaller investors, smaller projects, and take it to the smaller communities and outlying cities and towns as well?

4.1.2 Smaller investment companies

Once the requirement of being a bank to offer participatory financing is removed, there is no valid reason why the investment companies cannot be established on a smaller scale as well. In practice, they may be set up as private limited liability companies instead of as public limited companies. Then it will become possible to set up smaller investment companies in smaller communities catering to smaller investors and smaller projects. This will have enormous implications for local level economic development. For it will then become possible to extend the benefits of the scheme to provincial capitals and smaller cities.

In the previous chapter we conceived of a scheme whereby commercial banks will provide participatory financing to smaller entrepreneurs at the local level. However, they too will run into the same banking permission problem outside the few countries where Islamic banking is allowed. The smaller investment companies we have considered above should be able to offer an alternative where participatory financing through commercial banks is not allowed, and to complement and co-exist where it is permitted. In particular, it will open new vistas to smaller Muslim communities living in countries where financing will otherwise be available only on conventional terms.

There is a special advantage too in organising smaller investment companies. Since they can be started and operated without much difficulty, it looks a natural starting point to begin experimenting with the participatory financing scheme. If they fail the damage is minimal. If they succeed, then, with the experience and expertise acquired, and the confidence of the public gained, they can move up the ladder to become large and, eventually, convince the banking authorities and set up as investment banks.

The concerns we saw in the previous section fully apply to these companies too. In fact, the concerns become even more worrying as the size of the companies and their projects become smaller, since as the size decreases the resources available to them to mount a proper accounting, auditing and financial management system may become insufficient. In such a situation the success of the scheme will become crucially dependent on the honesty and integrity of the entrepreneurs and the companies.

The projects expected to be financed by these investment companies are pure profit-motivated economic enterprises. And they have to make sufficient profits to make it attractive even when the profits are distributed among the three players — the investor, the company and the entrepreneur. As such they should not be expected to engage in projects whose main aim is social development. Commercially financing such projects, as discussed in section 3.2.2, becomes viable only when commercial banks can participate with their credit creating privilege. In so far as many countries are not going to allow commercial banks to offer participatory financing, commercial financing of community projects and the resulting micro-level socio-economic development will remain the special privilege and advantage of the few that permit their banks to offer such schemes.

4.1.3 Pure mudaraba partnerships

As the project size decreases the turnover and profit will decrease, and a point will be reached when it will no longer be possible to pay for the services of the intermediary nor the profit sufficient to make the three-way split. Such projects, naturally, will not be attractive to any investment company. Is that the limit of the participatory financing scheme? Yes, but it may also be the beginning of pure mudaraba partnership, where the financier and the entrepreneur deal with each other directly, without the intermediary. Put in another way, participatory financing begins where pure mudaraba partnership leaves off. In fact they are different sections of the same spectrum catering to a wide range of different situations; the last capable of reaching and serving the needs of the very locality of the partners.

Pure mudaraba partnership is a person to person relationship, based on personal knowledge of the entrepreneur's capabilities and his honesty and integrity. Trust between the financier and the entrepreneur is the foundation on which such partnerships will be established and maintained or destroyed. If this mudaraba partnership is revived and helped to flourish, it will take the dream of economic prosperity through equal recognition of, and reward for, capital and labour several steps closer to fruition.

4.1.4 Concerns about controls

We have stressed throughout this section the importance of the honesty and integrity of the partners in the scheme for its success. We developed the whole participatory financing scheme as an alternative to financing by traditional interest-bearing investments and loans, on the assumption that Muslims — both as investors and as entrepreneurs — do not wish to deal in interest on account of their religious conviction and the fear of God. Such a Muslim is by definition honest and trustworthy. Therefore, if our assumption is correct, the scheme we have developed should necessarily succeed. *Insha Allah.* (God willing.) Yet all dealings should be made transparent by proper accounting and auditing. This is necessary in order to ensure the continued existence of the trust, for trust unsupported by verifiable facts is still suspect. If our assumption does not exist in any given place or time, or in a particular case, then the scheme is destined to fail and should not be attempted.

4.2 Credit expansion and economic development

Development, especially economic development, requires money. And money, either you have it or you must borrow it. Leaving aside public development activities and concerning ourselves with only private economic activities, the necessary capital can be raised from investors, creditors or the banks. The commercial banks provide capital in the form of loans and advances, and this is called bank credit. The economic development of a society is dependent, to a very large extent, on the availability of this bank credit to its business and entrepreneurial community. The fact that commercial banks can create credit and thereby make more "money" available than is otherwise possible, is an important factor in the economic development of any country.

The ultimate base for the total credit expansion capacity of the country as a whole is the reserve holdings of its central bank. However, this capacity is limited in practice by the circumstances in which the local commercial banks might find themselves. Specifically, they are constrained by four factors which are largely beyond their control but are dependent on the society they serve: 1. The size of the collateral available in the community that is acceptable to the banks, 2. The demand for credit, 3. The cash reserve ratio, and 4. The total legal tender (notes and coins and balances at the central bank) available to them as reserve. The scheme we have proposed helps expand the availability of this bank credit in less developed countries by easing these constraints in several ways. We will presently see how this works when commercial banks participate-finance projects and PF enterprises are established.

4.2.1 Collateral

The new PF enterprises have been established (i.e. buildings, machinery and equipment, working capital etc. have been acquired) using bank money. In a way money has been "lent" to the enterprise by the bank. Usually a commercial bank lends money to an enterprise or an individual only on the strength of a collateral that the borrower provides, and the size of the loan depends on the value of the collateral. But money was "lent" to this PF enterprise not on the strength of any existing collateral but the assets of the new enterprise acquired using the bank's "loan" itself has been pledged as collateral. In other words, the new PF enterprises, which did not exist before, themselves have become new collaterals. This takes place in both types of commercial bank PF projects — private enterprises as well as the community projects. Thus the PF scheme extends the capacity of the community to borrow by creating new collaterals for such borrowing.

4.2.2 Demand for credit

The new enterprises were established using venture capital provided by the PF funds. But they will need further financing, including short-term advances, for various normal business operations, and this creates new demand for credit. The demand created by the new economic activity will be met by the bank's existing reserves or it will seek and acquire additional reserves.

4.2.3 Cash reserve ratio

Both because the credit has to be drawn upon using cheques and because the PF scheme demands proper accounting, most of the transactions will take place through the bank. The prestige that goes with an enterprise that is financed by a bank — in fact where the bank is the main share holder — makes the enterprise's cheques widely acceptable, enabling it to deal with creditors more easily and without having to always pay for in cash. All these previously non-existent cheque-based transactions will help the bank to expand its ability to supply credit. For, since less cash is used in the transactions, bank's cash reserve ratio could be lowered to that extent enabling more credit to be extended on the same cash base.

4.2.4 Reserves

The banks' capacity to extend credit is also enhanced by the expansion of its cash base (reserves) in two ways. One, if the banks begin to show consistently good returns in their PF operations more people will bring in their savings to investment accounts. Two, the fact of seeing the PF projects helping their own local community — perhaps themselves too — directly may also encourage the local investors to bring in more of their capital and savings. Additionally, in the Muslim countries, the fact that they can employ their capital and savings to earn an income without involving in interest dealings — as in a time or savings deposit account in a conventional bank — also will help bring in funds previously unavailable to the banking system.

4.3 Considerations of liquidity

In our discussions so far we have assumed that once a cash deposit is made at a bank it can immediately create credit (i.e. grant loans and advances) equal to a multiple of the amount of the deposit. This assumption, however, does not generally hold in practice since there is now hardly any closed community served by only one single-office bank. People transact business outside the community as well, and the local bank, even if it is the only bank in the locality, is often a branch of a large bank. In Appendix B we have briefly explained the process of credit creation in one-bank and many-bank situations.

As we see in Appendix B, in practice, the bank lends only once on the strength of a deposit and that too an amount less than the deposit, not a multiple. However, it is done not only on incoming cash deposits but also on all incoming deposits of the cheques of other banks. For such a deposit immediately increases its reserves at the Central Bank. (Such is not the case when the cheque is from one customer to another of the same bank, because then it is only a book-entry operation at the bank and causes no increase in the reserve position.)

Since the reserve position is unaffected by the destination — i.e. whether it is a current account, savings account or an investment account — of a deposit, a deposit made into a PF investment account does not change anything in the credit creating process. Therefore the bank cannot immediately grant financing to a PF project to the full extent that the reserve ratio could be expected to allow on the strength of a PF deposit. It would take time while the credit creating process passes through the banking system, and it would also depend on the share this bank commands in the total cake of reserve funds. Fortunately, both these parameters — time and share — can be estimated from the bank's past data, and that should be used to guide in determining its future course.

In practice it means two things: One, the credit multiplier is not determined entirely by the reserve ratio and other factors we saw in theory,[6] but by still other factors as well which can be ascertained only by statistical studies of past data. Two, the time taken to attain the potential limit also can be estimated only from past data. These parameters, therefore, will vary from bank to bank and each has to determine its own parameters with sufficient margins to guarantee liquidity.

Consequently, while the bank can determine in advance the size of the financing it can provide based on a given deposit in the investment account, it cannot release all that amount immediately. That will depend on the time parameter and its share in the total banking business as well as on the demands made on the bank's reserves by its other regular activities such as loans and advances — both long term and short term.

As such the bank will have to exercise extreme caution, and release funds to the PF projects *gradually* in order not to jeopardise its liquidity position.

4.4 Project size

We have already seen that the size of an enterprise is an important factor in deciding on the type of financing it requires. There are large scale projects which require international or investment bank financing, and there are, at the other end of the spectrum, small one-man undertakings which are best financed by loans. Expected turnover of a project in the former category is capable of paying for all the financial and other services it uses up and to provide handsome returns to its many investors,

---

[6] Appendix B.

while one in the latter category hardly needs, nor is it able to pay for, such services. The returns are often not much more than sufficient to provide for the entrepreneur himself and his family. The projects that should be considered for participatory financing by commercial banks lie somewhere in the middle of this large spectrum.

The upper limit will be largely determined by the investment opportunities presented to the bank and its own capacity and willingness to take part in such projects. It is the lower end that should present some problem. To begin with, the project's turnover should be large enough to pay the salaries of those employed by the project including the entrepreneur himself, and to pay for professional services such as accounting and auditing which participatory financing necessarily requires, and the supervisory costs of the bank. On top of it the project has to show sufficient profits to retain the current investment and to attract further investment. But if this consideration pushes the limit far high, all the social benefits envisaged by the PF schemes will be lost, especially in the community projects.

Officers of the bank entrusted with making decisions on project financing will have to be fully aware of the conflicting interests and view them in proper perspective. General guidelines may be given by the top management but the mangers directly responsible for recommending PF financing should consider each case on its own merits with due regard to local conditions.

4.5 Education and training

The participatory financing scheme developed here is an entirely new concept. It is new in theory and new to those who will eventually participate in it — bankers, entrepreneurs and the investors. Therefore it is essential that it is fully understood by all concerned before any attempt is made at implementation. Both its philosophy as well as its practical aspects must be fully grasped. Bankers will have to develop methodologies and they have to, in turn, train their staff in their application. This will take time. Then potential entrepreneurs will have to be educated on the workings of the scheme, the advantages and the obligations. Finally potential investors will have to be convinced that this new scheme has something to offer them.

In less developed countries, providing short courses in banking-literacy for potential customers and in book-keeping for potential entrepreneurs will help greatly in successfully implementing the scheme. This, in turn, will go a long way in advancing national economic development. Perhaps third-world governments and local authorities might consider making some meaningful contribution in this area. Subsidising those teaching such courses is a practical step.

4.6 Conclusions

Participatory financing makes an important contribution to society in general; *viz.* it places labour — entre-preneurship, skill, talent, experience — on par with capital. To Muslims it offers two other very important additional openings. To those with capital it offers a way of earning a *halaal* income, and to the entrepreneur it opens access to *riba*-free capital which otherwise may not be possible.

Offering the PF scheme through investment banks and investment companies brings the benefit of the scheme to different investor-entrepreneur groups, to different levels of economic activity and to different geographical layers. Investment banks and larger investment companies would cater to large investors and operate at national and international levels, while the smaller investment companies will cater to smaller investors and operate at the local level. At the lowest level it may even bring about the revival of the pure form of *mudaraba* — that is, participatory financing without the intermediary. However, as we move away from the supervisory controls of the banking authorities and down the economic and geographical layers, the level of personal integrity, honesty and trust required of the entrepreneur (including the intermediary) increases. The success of the scheme depends squarely on the strength of their integrity.

Participatory financing by commercial banks is a very promising scheme both for the investor and the entrepreneur, as well as for the community. Whether the bank is an interest-free bank or a conventional interest-based one is immaterial to its practice. But its implementation should be tempered by the concerns raised in the preceding sections. A slow and cautious approach is recommended.

It is necessary to point out that participatory financing is not an alternative to conventional loans and advances. The latter serve a purpose that will continue to be a necessary part of any economic activity, irrespective of the presence or otherwise of participatory financing schemes.

It is also appropriate at this point to remind again that participatory financing is an *option* that commercial banks *may* embark upon. In particular, interest-free commercial banking[7] can be practised without embarking on participatory financing. Such a bank will be able to provide all commercial banking services provided by conventional banks, including conventional loans and advances, without any loss to its earnings on account of being interest-free. Only that it will pay no interest on deposits and therefore need not collect such interest from the borrowers and pass it onto the depositors. The advantage is: the cost of borrowing from an interest-free bank will be less than that of borrowing from a conventional one. Furthermore, such a commercial bank should have no difficulty in obtaining authorisation to operate in any country.

---

[7] As presented in Gafoor (1995).

Chapter 5

Effects of Inflation

In the previous chapters we discussed the participatory financing scheme ignoring inflation. But inflation has become a fact of life in all countries in the last few decades, and its magnitude is generally much higher and its effects more severe in the developing countries where most of the Muslims find themselves. As such it is necessary to study the effects of inflation on participatory financing. Our concern here is the *effects* of inflation; we will not attempt to define inflation or measure it; nor will we attempt to examine ways of counteracting it. They are the subject of a forthcoming publication. The present effort is only to understand how and where the effects are felt and to evaluate the extent of the damage. In the process, perhaps, we might tumble upon a method of damage control.

Inflation affects our scheme in two different ways — one directly and the other indirectly. We will consider them in turn.

5.1 Direct effects

The direct effect of inflation is mainly on the profit/loss share of the partners in the participatory financing scheme. Here we will try to identify and evaluate this effect. To begin with, the effects on commercial bank schemes will be different from the effects on investment bank schemes. Therefore let us consider them separately.

5.1.1 Commercial bank schemes

Let us now return to our example in Chapter 2 where $1000 of the investor's money was made into $9000 of bank money and invested in a project. In Table 1 we saw the distribution of profit/loss to the partners given the size of the profit/loss in nominal terms. Now we assume the presence of 15% inflation and see what difference it makes to their shares. Table 3 gives the scenarios when inflation is present. The first line of each scenario gives the distribution in nominal values; the second line gives the situation after adjusting for 15 percent inflation. The scenarios go from 10 percent nominal profit to 5 percent nominal loss in steps of 5 percent.

Suppose the project made a profit of $900. This is 10% in nominal terms. Dividing the profit equally among the partners, each will get $300 — scenario 1. This will be a net gain to the bank and the entrepreneur. The investor, however, will receive less than this because his original investment in the meantime would have lost some of its value due to inflation. In this case his $1000 would have lost $150 (15%) and therefore, after compensating for this loss, his net gain would be only $150 — scenario 1a. When the project's profit is 5 percent the investor's profit rate becomes equal to the inflation rate and he makes no more net gain — scenarios 2, 2a. This critical value (5%) depends on several factors: inflation rate, investor's share in the profit and the credit creating factor of the bank. See Appendix A, equation 17.

We see that as long as the investor's profit rate is not less than the inflation rate none of the partners suffer any loss. But once equality is reached, though the investor gains the same profit as the others, his gain is lost when adjusted for inflation. The others do not suffer this loss (due to inflation) because they had no investment of their own to begin with.

When there is no profit in nominal terms, the investor suffers a net loss to the extent of the inflation rate — scenario 3a. The bank suffers loss only when there is a loss in nominal terms — scenario 4; the loss to the investor in this case is very high — scenario 4a. The entrepreneur suffers no loss under any scenario.

Table 3. Profit/loss distribution among the partners
(Investment: $1000 cash, providing $9000 in bank money)
(In the presence of 15 percent inflation)

Scen-ario	Project		Investor		Bank	Entre-preneur
	Amount	%	Amount	%	Amount	Amount
1.	900	10	300	30	300	300
1a.*			150**	15	300	300
2.	450	5	150	15	150	150
2a.			0	0	150	150
3.	0	0	0	0	0	0
3a.			-150	-15	0	0
4.	-450	-5	-225	-22.5	-225	0
4a.			-375	-37.5	-225	0
Share in:						
profit	1		1/3		1/3	1/3
loss	1		1/2		1/2	0

* Adjusted for 15 percent inflation   ** 300 - 150 [= 15% of 1000]

Under inflationary conditions, then, the entrepreneur and the bank gain the same way as they did when there was no inflation — the former never loses and the bank loses only when there is a loss. The investor's gains are more tempered, while his losses are more accentuated. This is entirely due to the erosion of his capital due to inflation. When there is no loss to the project in nominal terms, his entire loss is due to this factor alone. In that case the loss he suffered would be the same as if he kept his capital with himself or deposited with a bank in a non-interest-bearing account.

5.1.2 Investment bank schemes

Table 3 represents the effects in the general scheme, which is applicable to participatory financing by commercial banks. When the participatory financing is done by an investment bank, it will take the form in Table 4. Here too the scenarios go from 10 percent nominal profit to 5 percent nominal loss in steps of 5 percent. (Note that here the shares are distributed slightly differently from Table 3.) In scenarios 1 and 2, all the partners have nominal profits. But the investor's profit when adjusted for his capital loss due to inflation becomes a loss in real terms while others are not so affected — scenarios 1a and 2a. In scenarios 3 and 3a, the project records no profit in nominal terms and so none of the partners receive any profit, but the investor suffers capital loss to the full extent of inflation. When the project records a loss then both the bank and the investor suffer losses while the entrepreneur is not affected — scenario 4. The investor's real loss is much heavier — scenario 4a. This is due to two reasons: one, his share in the loss is double that of the bank and, two, he also bears the full capital erosion.

Table 4. Profit/loss distribution among the partners
(Investment: $9000 cash)
(In the presence of 15 percent inflation)

Scen-ario	Project		Investor		Bank	Entre-preneur
	Amount	%	Amount	%	Amount	Amount
1.	900	10	400	4.44	200	300
1a.*			-950**	-10.55	200	300
2.	450	5	200	2.22	100	150
2a.			-1150	-12.77	100	150
3.	0	0	0	0	0	0
3a.			-1350	-15.00	0	0
4.	-450	-5	-300	-3.33	-150	0
4a.			-1650	-18.33	-150	0
Share in:						
profit	**1**		**4/9**		**2/9**	**3/9**
loss	**1**		**2/3**		**1/3**	**0**
5.	1350	15	600	6.66	300	450
5a.			-750	-8.33	300	450
6.	3037.5	33.75	1350	15	675	1012.5
6a.			0	0	675	1012.5

* Adjusted for 15 percent inflation   ** 400 - 1350 [= 15% of 9000]

When does the investor gain a profit in real terms? In scenario 6 he gains a profit equal to that of the erosion of his capital due to inflation. His rate of profit this time is

15%, the same as inflation. But when adjusted for inflation he neither gains nor loses. This is his threshold point. This threshold point is attained when the project makes a nominal profit of 33.75 percent. For the investor to receive any real profit the project must reach a profit rate above this. The point to note from Table 4 is that, in the presence of inflation, projects under investment bank schemes have to attain very high profit rates if the investor is to get any reasonable profit. Compare Tables 3 and 4.

5.2 Indirect effects

We saw in the previous section that so long as the profit rate of the investor is not less than the inflation rate everyone stands to gain. Once this threshold point is reached, the first to lose is the investor. Then, he has two options: to continue to hold onto his investment account, hoping that things will improve next time around, or to shift his funds to a deposit account where his capital is guaranteed. Here again he faces a dilemma. If the bank is an interest-free bank, then while the nominal value of his capital is guaranteed, inflation would erode its real value to the extent of inflation. In this case he is better off staying with the investment account even after reaching the threshold point, for this would still be less damaging than the loss suffered due to inflation by transferring to a deposit account. In fact he would still be better off so long as the profit rate of the project is not less than zero because it is at the latter point that his loss will be equal to the capital erosion due to inflation.

For example, if he put 1000 in the deposit account and received 1000 at the end of one year (under capital guarantee) and the inflation rate during the period was 15 percent, the real value of his original capital would now be

850. On the other hand, if he had this 1000 in an investment account and there was no nominal profit, his capital would now be worth the same 850 in real terms (case 3a, Table 3).

To the bank this means that so long as it does not make any loss, on the average, its customers in the investment accounts will stay with it. When it shows loss they would prefer to switch their funds to deposit accounts, if not elsewhere. At the same time, since a loss would have to be shared by the bank as well, it would suffer capital losses. Hence the bank would have to terminate all its participatory financing operations if it cannot show any profit.

The other side of the coin is that if the investment accounts make at least no loss, the deposit account holders would be better off switching their funds to investment accounts. Because, compared to sure erosion of their capital in the deposit accounts due to inflation, here there is a chance that this erosion will at least be partially compensated. This, however, has a serious consequence. For it will dry up funds available for ordinary bank lending, which is very essential for keeping the existing businesses running and for financing small businesses. Thus, in the presence of inflation, even a minimal success of participatory financing can be bad news for normal commercial bank lending. Proper solution, of course, lies in preventing the capital erosion in the first place. Either remove inflation or compensate for the loss. A possible solution for the latter is the subject of a forthcoming publication.

The dilemma, however, will continue even after a solution is found for capital erosion due to inflation. In the long run, the system will settle down to a natural balance when the types of deposits and their uses are matched by the intentions of the depositors. That is, when those whose main aim is to use their capital to earn an income go to investment accounts and these funds are used in PF operations, and those whose main aim is to have their savings safe go to (non-interest-bearing-but-capital-guaranteed) savings accounts and these funds are used by the bank to grant loans and advances to small businesses and running concerns as well as for consumption purposes. In the meantime, perhaps the Central Bank has to step in to maintain a healthy rationing between the two forms of financing.

In case the customers have a choice of interest-free banks and interest-paying banks and wish to safeguard any loss to the real worth of their capital, they would begin to consider (ignoring internal and/or external compulsion to abide by the *riba* prohibition rule) switching over to a deposit account in a conventional bank once the threshold point is reached. In such a situation if the interest paid by the bank is more than the rate of inflation, they would be better off making the switch over — at least they can safeguard the real value of their capital.

This means, to a bank offering investment accounts on the basis of participatory financing, that it has to make a profit in its PF operations at least to the extent of compensating the investors for the capital erosion they suffer due to inflation if it is not to lose its investment account customers and their funds.

5.3 Compensation for value erosion of capital

If we take the position that the entrepreneur and the bank are compensated for their time and work by way of salary etc. and the profit is for their initiative and responsibility, then it may stand to reason to compensate the investor for the sure loss he suffers due to inflation. One way of doing it would be to consider the erosion of investor capital due to inflation as part of project expenses and compute the profit net of this amount. In this case the investor's account will be credited first with an amount equal to the capital erosion, and then the remaining profit will be shared among the partners. Then all three partners will stand on the same level ground. If capital is so guaranteed that would encourage people to deposit their excess funds in investment accounts with the bank and prevent those already in investment accounts moving to savings accounts. It will also take away the excuse some have for depositing their funds in banks where savings accounts earn an interest income saying that it is compensation for their loss due to inflation. This is also much less complicated — for the computations as well as for understanding and explaining.

The profit/loss distribution for commercial bank schemes when the project's profit/loss is computed after compensating for the investor's capital loss due to inflation is given in Table 5. (Note that the compensation is for the *investor's capital loss*, not that of the project. Thus, in our examples, it is 15% of 1000 in the case of the commercial bank scheme and 15% of 9000 in the case of the investment bank scheme.) The second lines (1b, 2b, etc.) in each scenario represent this distribution. The first lines (1a, 2a, etc.) in each scenario is the same as the corresponding second lines in Table 3. This is intended to make comparing the distributions under the different regimes easy. The corresponding distribution in investment bank schemes is given in Table 6.

**Table 5. Distribution when profit/loss is computed
"net" of inflation**
(Investment: $1000 cash, providing $9000 in bank money.
Inflation: 15%)

Scen-ario	Project		Investor		Bank	Entre-preneur
	Amount	%	Amount	%	Amount	Amount
1a.	900	10	150*	15	300	300
1b.	750**		250	25	250	250
2a.	450	5	0	0	150	150
2b.	300		100	10	100	100
3.	0	0	-150	-15	0	0
3a.	-150		-75	-7.5	-75	0
4a.	-450	-5	-375	-37.5	-225	0
4b.	-600		-300	-30	-300	0
Share in:						
profit	1		1/3		1/3	1/3
loss	1		1/2		1/2	0
5a.	150	1.66	-100	-10	50	50
5b.	0		0	0	0	0

* (1/3)(900) - 150 [= 15% of 1000]   ** 900 - 150 [=15% of 1000]

Note: First line (in each scenario) represents distribution when the
profit/loss is in nominal terms and the investor's share is given
adjusted for his capital loss due to inflation. (Same as the second line
in Table 3). Second line gives the distribution when "net" profit is
used. This is computed by deducting (from the nominal profit) the loss
(to investor's capital) due to inflation.

Table 6. Distribution when profit/loss is computed
net of inflation
(Investment: $9000 cash. Inflation: 15%)

Scenario	Project		Investor		Bank	Entrepreneur
	Amount	%	Amount	%	Amount	Amount
1a.	900	10	-950*	-10.55	200	300
1b.	-450**		-300	-3.33	-150	0
2a.	450	5	-1150	-12.77	100	150
2b.	-900		-600	- 6.66	-300	0
3a.	0	0	-1350	-15.00	0	0
3b.	-1350		-900	-10	-450	0
4a.	-450	-5	-1650	-18.33	-150	0
4b.	-1800		-1200	-13.33	-600	0
Share in:						
profit	1		4/9		2/9	3/9
loss	1		2/3		1/3	0
5a.	1350	15	-750	-8.33	300	450
5b.	0		0	0	0	0
6a.	3037.5	33.75	0	0	675	1012.5
6b.	1687.5		750	8.33	375	562.5

* (4/9)(900) - 1350 [= 15% of 9000]   ** 900 - 1350 [= 15% of 9000]

Note: First line (in each scenario) represents distribution when the profit/loss is in nominal terms and the investor's share is given adjusted for loss of his capital due to inflation. (Same as the second line in Table 4). Second line gives the distribution when net profit is used. This is computed by deducting (from the nominal profit) the loss (to investor's capital — here same as project capital) due to inflation.

The first thing one notices in these tables is that the profit of the investor in each case is increased while his losses are reduced. This, of course, comes at the expense of the other two partners. But the question is which of the two distributions is more equitable.

Under the new regime, all the partners will reach the threshold point (*i.e.* when they make no profit or loss) at the same time. See scenarios 5b in both tables. In addition, the threshold point is reached at a much lower nominal profit rate than under the other regime. In the case of commercial banks, it is when the nominal profit is 1.66 percent[1] as opposed to 5 percent. See scenarios 5b and 2a in Table 5. In the case of investment banks it is at 15 percent — same as the inflation rate — as compared to 33.75 percent. See scenarios 5b and 6a in Table 6.

In fact, the profit/loss distribution will revert to those found in Tables 1 and 2 when the profit/loss is computed net of investor capital erosion due to inflation. We recommend this approach.

5.4 Conclusions

What we have shown as the effects of inflation are only indicative. However, what emerges from this cursory investigation is that inflation has no worse consequence on capital when deposited in a PF investment account than when that same money is kept idle or deposited in a non-interest-bearing account so long as there is a profit, in nominal terms, on all the PF operations of the bank as a whole, however small that may be.

---

[1] This figure is obtained by dividing the rate of inflation by the credit multiplying factor of the bank. See Appendix A, eqn. 28.

We have also seen that in the presence of inflation, investment bank financed projects will have to achieve much higher levels of profit, compared to their commercial bank counterparts financed with the same amount of project capital, before the investor can begin to record profits. The commercial bank's advantage in this respect is entirely due to its credit creating ability.

In both cases, considering the erosion of investor capital as part of project expenses and reimbursing this amount to the investor (or rather to the project) before distributing the resulting profit/loss to the partners will prove a better and more equitable approach.

Finally, projects participate-financed by investment banks will begin to provide profits to all three partners so long as their nominal rates keep up with the rate of inflation. The required rate is only a fraction of the inflation rate in the case of commercial bank participate-financed projects. This fraction depends on the bank's credit multiplying factor.

Chapter 6

Summary and Conclusion

People posses two types of money. One, that is spent on regular or immediate needs, and the other, that is not required for such use. The latter can be deployed in different ways, including just keeping it safe, lending it, and investing it. We have looked at the usual ways in which these purposes are generally achieved and their acceptability in Islam. We identified the money used for earning an income as concerning us in this study. Realising this aim without dealing in interest leaves one with only one option: investment — in one's own enterprise, in partnership with one or more others, or in a *mudaraba* type participation where the investor is a sleeping partner.

In a small community where everyone knows nearly everyone and where the investment involved is within the means of one or two or a small number of persons known to and trusting each other, this works well. But when the community becomes large and where people no longer know each other well and where the capital involved runs into large sums, the limits of this system shows up. This is where the bank comes into the picture; it becomes an intermediary between the investor and the entrepreneur. The concept of investment accounts and the use of funds from these accounts to finance projects on a *mudaraba* basis was introduced into commercial banking by the Islamic banks. This should work well if only new projects were financed using only the funds from the investment accounts. Problems arose when the same concept was applied where lending was appropriate and where funds from other accounts were employed.

To the basic concepts of investment accounts and *mudaraba* participation we added the credit creating ability of the commercial banks and developed the concept of participatory financing. We also developed a mechanism for implementing the concept. On examining the practical aspects of implementing the mechanism we discovered that larger investors and larger projects had characteristics different from those of the smaller investors and smaller projects. The former combination suited the investment banks and therefore we have argued for the recognition of this fact and for the establishment of investment banks to cater to this group of investors. The smaller investors and smaller projects may well be served by commercial banks but under certain conditions.

Participatory financing by commercial banks is well suited to one category of borrowers who are traditionally catered to by commercial bank loans: the entrepreneurs investing in new enterprises. The other categories should still be catered to by traditional forms of loans and advances, but with the difference that the funds come from non-interest-bearing deposits whose capital is guaranteed, and the borrowers are charged a fee for the services.

Among the new enterprises that can be participate-financed by commercial banks there are two types. One where the prime objective is to earn an income and profit, and the other where the primary aim is to provide services aimed at the economic and social development of the community but financed and run on a commercial basis. It is envisaged that both these types of enterprises will be based mainly in the geographical locality of the participating banks and therefore will essentially benefit and develop the local economy; the second type specially catering to the rural and less developed sections of the community.

So far so good. But there are situations where the banks may not be allowed to or are unable to offer participatory financing schemes. Offering the same through investment companies seems to be appropriate in these instances. We have looked at the pros and cons of these as well as that offered through the banks in a separate chapter.

We have also studied the effects of inflation on our schemes. It appears that considering the value erosion of capital due to inflation as part of project expenses and crediting this amount to the investor (or rather the project) before the "net" profit/loss is computed and distributed among the partners seems a good solution.

In this short essay we have tried to look at the use of funds available for investment, in perspective. By studying the characteristics of the different types of funds, people, projects and banks, we developed a conceptual framework where the different components find fitting places. The spectrum is large and varied. As such we have drawn only an overview, and have limited ourselves to conceptual issues. The practical aspects have to be worked out both in their generality and in their specifics. This larger undertaking will require considerable resources including academic and professional expertise and experience.

Appendix A

Mathematical Relationships

The profit/loss distributions in the tables in the text were computed using numerical values. We will present here the mathematical relationships among the variables so that the profit/loss distributions for various different combinations of the variables could be easily computed. These can also be used to arrive at optimum combinations in given situations as well as to do simulation studies.

Our first aim is to find expressions for the profits of the three partners in terms of their respective agreed-upon shares in the profit, the profit rate achieved by the project, investor's capital and the credit multiplying (or credit creating) factor of the bank. We will also find an expression for the profit rate of the investor in terms of the other variables. Also for his net profit and profit rate in the presence of inflation. We will also find a general expression for the profit rate of the project below which the investor will begin to lose. Secondly, analysing these relationships we will derive some general conclusions.

A0. Some notations and definitions

Let SB be the agreed-upon share of the profit due to the bank
  SE „   „   „   the entrepreneur
  SI „   „   „   the investor

and let PP\$ be the profit achieved by the project (in dollars)

    PB\$ be the profit due to the bank (in dollars)
    PE\$ „   the entrepreneur (in dollars)
    PI\$ „   the investor (in dollars).

Then,

(1)   PB$=   SB*PP$
(2)   PE$=   SE*PP$
(3)   PI$=   SI*PP$

subject to the condition

(4)   SB+SE+SI = 1

since the shares of the partners must sum up to 1.

Let   KI\$ be the capital invested by the investor (in dollars)
and   CM be the credit multiplying factor used by the
commercial bank.[1]

Then,   KB$ the capital invested by the bank is given
by the relationship

(5)   KB$=   CM*KI$

A1. Profits

If   PP   is the profit rate achieved by the project, then

(6)   PP$=   PP*KB$.

---

[1]   CM is primarily related to the cash reserve ratio (CR). In its simplest form CM = (1/CR - 1). Thus when CR=10%, CM = 100/10 - 1 = 9; when CR=5, CM=19, and when CR=100, CM=0. Thus when the cash reserve ratio is 100 percent no credit can be created, while as the CR decreases the ability to create credit increases. However, the reserves we have been talking about so far is the reserves legally required by the central bank, and this has to be maintained at all times and this cannot be used when cash withdrawal is demanded. Therefore banks have to have additional reserves to cater to this daily contingency. This increases the actual reserve ratio maintained by the banks. There are other reasons too, including the bank's desire to maintain a safe margin. Consequently, the effective credit multiplier is much smaller.

For an extensive but very readable treatment, see Hutchinson (1992), chs. 11 and 12.

From (1) and (6),

(7)   PB$= SB*PP*KB$

and from (7) and (5),

(8)   PB$= SB*PP*CM*KI$.

Similarly,

(9)   PE$= SE*PP*CM*KI$ and

(10)   PI$= SI*PP*CM*KI$.

Results 1

a) PB$, PE$ and PI$ are directly proportional to PP, CM and KI$. That is, increasing the project's profit rate, the bank's credit multiplying factor or the capital of the investor, individually or severally, will proportionately increase the profits of all three partners. The converse is also true, i.e. decrease in any one will result in decrease in the profits.

b) Increase in the share of any one partner will also increase his profits, but that will be at the expense of the others, since the sum of the profits must add up to the total.

A2. Profit rates

Let the profit rates attained by the bank, the entrepreneur and the investor be PB, PE and PI respectively.

Let PB be defined as   PB = PB$/KB$

        PE   ,,   PE = PE$/KB$

and PI   ,,   PI = PI$/KI$.

Then,

$$(11) \quad PB = PB\$/KB\$ = SB*PP\$/KB\$$$
$$= SB*PP*KB\$/KB\$$$
$$= SB*PP.$$

Similarly,

$$(12) \quad PE = SE*PP.$$

But, $\quad PI = SI*PP*KB\$/KI\$$
$$= SI*PP*CM*KI\$/KI\$.$$

Therefore

$$(13) \quad PI = SI*PP*CM.$$

Results 2

a) Profit rates of the partners are directly proportional to the profit rate of the project. That is, if the project achieves high profit rates the rates of the partners are also proportionately increased. The reverse also holds true.

b) Increase in the share of any one partner will also increase his profit rate, but that will be at the expense of the others, since the sum of the shares must add up to 1.

c) The profit rate of the investor, however, is directly proportional to the credit multiplying factor as well. Hence investor's profit rate can be increased by investing with a bank that has higher credit multiplying factor.

A3. Profits in the presence of inflation

Let the rate of inflation be INF, the net profit (in dollars) of the investor (i.e. after compensating for the loss suffered by his capital due to inflation) be PIN\$ and the rate PIN.

Then, $\text{PIN\$} = \text{PI\$} - \text{INF}*\text{KI\$}$

(14) $= \text{SI}*\text{PP}*\text{CM}*\text{KI\$} - \text{INF}*\text{KI\$}$

Therefore, $\text{PIN} = \text{PIN\$}/\text{KI\$}$

$= \text{SI}*\text{PP}*\text{CM} - \text{INF}$

(15) $\text{PIN} = \text{PI} - \text{INF}$

Results 3

a) The net profit of the investor in the presence of inflation (PIN\$) depends on his investment and the inflation rate, besides his agreed-upon share in the profit, the profit rate of the project and the credit multiplying factor of the bank.

b) His net profit rate is equal to his nominal profit rate less the inflation rate.

A4. Threshold point

Let the threshold point PP' be defined as the profit rate of the project when the net profit rate of the investor is zero, *i.e.* when PIN = 0.

At this point equation 15 reduces to

(16) $\text{PI} = \text{INF}.$

That is, the threshold point PP' is reached when the profit rate of the investor is equal to the inflation rate.

Then, since $\text{PI} = \text{SI}*\text{PP}*\text{CM}$ (eqn. 13)

the threshold point PP' is given by

(17) $\text{PP'} = \text{INF}/(\text{SI}*\text{CM}).$

Results 4

a) The threshold point is directly proportional to the inflation rate and inversely proportional to the investor's share and the bank's credit multiplying factor.

b) If inflation is zero, the threshold point is zero.

A5. The case of investment banks

So far we have derived expressions and conclusions for the general case. They are directly applicable to the commercial bank schemes. Since investment banks cannot create credit, they cannot finance projects with bank money as the commercial banks do. Instead they use the deposit itself. Then, the CM we have been using so far becomes *effectively* one (instead of zero) and hence the investment bank scheme becomes a special case of the general scheme with CM=1. Let us now study the implications.

When CM=1, equation (5) becomes

(18)   KB$ = KI$,

(i.e. the capital invested in the project by the investment bank is exactly the same as the investor's deposit.)

and equations 8, 9 and 10 giving the profits of the partners become, respectively

(19)   PB$ = SB*PP*KI$
(20)   PE$ = SE*PP*KI$ and
(21)   PI$ = SI*PP*KI$.

Equation (13) giving the profit rate of the investor becomes

(22)   PI = SI*PP.

His profit rate net of inflation given by equation 15 remains the same,

and equation (17) giving the threshold point becomes

(23) $\qquad$ PP' = INF/SI.

Results 5

a) An investment bank cannot finance projects to any amount greater than the cash available in its investment accounts. (cf. equations 5 and 18.)

b) Consequently, the profits attained by the partners in an investment bank financed project are several times less than that attained by a commercial bank funded project using the same amount of investor capital. (cf. eqns. 8, 9 and 10 with eqns. 19, 20 and 21.)

c) So is the profit rate of the investor. (cf. eqns. 13 and 22.)

d) In the presence of inflation, the threshold point PP' is given by equations 17 and 23. The value of PP' in the former is several times smaller than that in the latter, since eqn. 17 has CM in the denominator. In plain words, a project financed by an investment bank has to attain a profit rate several times higher than one financed by a commercial bank, before it can reach the no-loss level for the investor.

e) The threshold point could be decreased by increasing the share of the investor, and its value is equal to the rate of inflation divided by the share of the investor. (Eqn. 23)

f) Since any share is always less than one, the threshold point in an investment bank scheme is always greater than the rate of inflation.

A6. When profit is calculated net of inflation

It was suggested in section 5.3 that the investor be compensated for the erosion of his capital before the rest of the profit/loss is apportioned among the partners. We will see below the consequences of that approach.

Let PPN\$ be the "net" profit of the project, i.e. after compensating the investor for the erosion of his capital due to inflation, and PPN be the rate for such profit.

Then,   PPN\$ = PP\$ - INF*KI\$

and   PPN   = PPN\$/KB\$
                = PP\$/KB\$ - INF*KI\$/KB\$
                = PP - INF/CM,

on account of eqns. 5 and 6.
i.e.
(24)   PPN= PP - INF/CM.

The profits of the partners in this case (PBN\$, PEN\$, PIN\$) can be easily arrived at from the basic equations or by substituting PPN for PP in equations 8, 9 and 10 as follows:

(25)   PBN\$ = SB*KI\$*(PP*CM - INF)

(26)   PEN\$ = SE*KI\$*(PP*CM - INF)

(27)   PIN\$ = SI*KI\$*(PP*CM - INF).

When   (PP*CM - INF) = 0, all three equations become zero. That is, the threshold point is reached simultaneously. And this point is given by,

(28)   PPN' = INF/CM.

Results 6

a) Since all three equations (25, 26 and 27) have the same common factor, the net profits of the partners (in terms of dollars) is directly proportional to their respective agreed-upon shares.

b) For the same reason, they all arrive at their threshold (no-loss-no-gain) point at the same time.

c) PPN' is much lower than PP' since the latter has SI, which is always less than 1, in the denominator. (cf. eqns. 17 and 28.)

d) Under this arrangement, the threshold point for projects financed by investment banks is equal to the rate of inflation. (Since CM=1, in eqn. 28.)

A7. Loss distribution

Under our participatory financing scheme, when

PP > 0, all three partners share the profit according to a set of pre-fixed ratios;

PP = 0, no partner gains or loses;

PP < 0, the entrepreneur shares no part of the loss, and the other two partners share the loss according to another set of pre-fixed ratios.

Results 7

a) Given that SBL and SIL are the agreed-upon shares of the bank and the investor respectively in case of loss, and where SBL + SIL = 1,

(29) PB\$ = SBL*PP\$,
(30) PE\$ = 0, and
(31) PI\$ = SIL*PP\$ when PP < 0.

b) When the profit is calculated net of inflation, The same equations (29, 30 and 31) will hold, except that instead of PP\$ we will then use PPN\$ in the computations.

Appendix B

Explanation of some banking terms and processes

Some of the banking terms and processes used in the text are briefly explained here. The uninitiated might find it necessary. They could actually be footnotes but since some are quite lengthy and therefore may distract the reader from the flow of the main story, especially in his first reading, we collected them all together and give as an appendix.

B1. Deposits and liabilities; reserve ratio and credit creation; loans and assets

When a bank grants loans, such as the $9000 mentioned in the text in section 2.1.3, it is not directly handed out in cash; nor does it occur in one step. Briefly, the process is as follows: When a customer deposits $1000 in cash, the bank creates a deposit entry in his favour which is a liability for the bank. The borrower may now draw cheques up to this amount. The bank's cash reserve has now increased by $1000 but it also has increased its liability by $1000. However, if the cash reserve ratio is 10 percent, the bank need to hold only $100 in cash reserve against this liability, and therefore has $900 excess reserve which it can advance as loan.

This is because although the customer has the right to draw cheques for all his $1000, it is expected, by long observed behaviour of customers, that only about 10% of it will be demanded in cash; all others will be in cheque-based transactions which will eventually cancel out when the recipients of these cheques deposit them in their accounts. They too will draw their own cheques on the strength of these deposits and their recipients too will subsequently deposit these cheques into their accounts cancelling out the earlier entry. This process is expected to go on without any cash more than about 10% being withdrawn on any deposit. Thus the remaining 90%, i.e. $900, is expected to be unused and therefore available for granting loans to other customers.

When another customer is granted a loan on the basis of this excess reserve, again the bank does not directly provide him with cash, but creates a current account deposit in his favour for the amount of the loan. The current account deposit it has created is a liability for the bank but this is balanced by an asset entry in favour of the bank which earns an income (by way of interest) for the bank. Suppose all this $900 is now advanced as loan to (one or more) customer(s) the corresponding current account deposit(s) liabilities must be supported by 10% of this $900, i.e. $90. (The assumption here is that the borrower will not demand all his loan in cash but will make his payments to his creditors by cheque. They in turn will make their transactions using cheques. So people will pay and receive but when the cheques reach the bank they cause only book-keeping operations — no cash reaches or leaves the vaults of the bank. Only in about 10% — the reserve ratio — of these cases are cheques expected to be presented to the bank for cash withdrawal which will be easily covered by the cash reserves held by the bank.) This leaves $810 as excess reserve, on which the bank can again advance further loans. So it goes on *ad infinitum*. When all the reserves are thus used up it can be shown that the total loans advanced comes up close to $9000.

The above, however, is a simplified scenario because we have tacitly assumed the existence of only one bank. This may still be so in a small closed community. But more usually there are many banks and one bank's cheque is regarded as good as cash by the other banks and when the second bank deposits it with the Central Bank[1] the first bank's reserves at the Central Bank is immediately reduced by that amount. So the first bank's reserve becomes the reserve of the second bank and it is the latter which will advance loans on the strength of it.

So in a many-bank situation the bank which received the cash deposit in the first place does not get to create all the potential credit. However, this bank also becomes the recipient of other banks' reserves, and creates credit on the strength of cash originally deposited in other banks. Thus wherever the original cash deposit takes place, it becomes the reserve base of the entire banking system and it is the banking system as a whole which creates the maximum possible credit — granting loans and acquiring interest earning assets.[2] Who gets what share of the cake depends largely on the distribution of the account-holders and the characteristics of their accounts. That is, the number of customers in each bank and the type of accounts they hold and the size and speed of the volume of transaction.

In practice, each bank treats the cash and other-bank cheques it receives as fresh cash, independent of its origins and, keeping the required cash reserves, lends the excess — but only once.

---

[1] Central Bank is the banker's bank.
[2] See Hutchinson (1992) for a good description of credit creation in a many-bank situation.

B2. Money supply; bank money;
creation and destruction of bank money

Money supply, in its narrow sense, is defined as the total of notes and coins in the hands of the public (i.e. outside the banks) and the demand deposits held by the public in commercial banks. This is generally denoted by M1. We will stick to this definition in our present discussions. This "money supply" money is what is available to the public for spending.

When some member of the public brings in some cash into the bank the money supply is immediately reduced by that amount because notes and coins from outside the bank has come inside the bank. If the money is deposited into a current account, the bank will immediately create a demand deposit entry in his favour for the same amount, and the money supply figure is immediately restored to its original value.[3] That is, this operation of depositing some cash into one's current account does not change the money supply. Looked at it another way, since a cheque drawn on the strength of a demand deposit with a bank is as good as notes and coins, the spending power of the public has not changed. The reverse process takes place when a cheque is presented at the bank and notes and coins are withdrawn, but here too no change occurs to the money supply.

The situation, however, is very different when the bank creates a demand deposit entry in its books in favour of a member of the public when granting him a loan. In this case there is no simple exchange of cash for demand deposit — generating no change in money supply — but

---

[3] Depositing into a savings account is dealt with later.

the money supply has suddenly been increased by the creation of the demand deposit entry.

This demand deposit entry can now be used, by drawing a cheque, to buy goods and services as if it were cash or to draw cash itself from the bank. A cheque can be passed on from hand to hand as if it were cash or deposited into the payee's account — crediting his account and debiting the drawer's — creating only book entry changes in the bank. For all practical purposes, then, this bank created money (or bank money) is as good as notes and coins. It should be noted at this point that the *use* of the bank money does not cause any new changes in the money supply.

The borrower does not own the demand deposit he is permitted to make use of, but owes it to the bank and has to repay this loan. He can do so in one of two ways — by cash or by writing a cheque in favour of the bank itself. When he pays by cash, he brings in notes and coins that were outside the bank thus reducing the money supply. The "money" that was created by the granting of a loan is now destroyed by the repayment of it. In the bank's books its earning assets (loan) entry is reduced and its cash reserve is increased. The liability side of its books is unaffected by this transaction; but the money supply is reduced by cash outside the bank coming inside. If he pays by cheque, the bank's earning assets are reduced as before but now the books are balanced by the destruction of the created money through the bank's liability (demand deposit) being reduced. The money supply is changed by this reduction in demand deposit, instead of by cash coming in from outside.

Money supply (M1) is the total "money" available to the community for immediate spending — part of it is its own and the rest is borrowed from the banks. The latter is called bank money.

We will now take up the case when notes and coins brought into the bank is deposited in a savings account instead of a current account. This money, though still owned by the depositor, is now not available to him for immediate spending. The money has left the "hands of the public" and gone into the vaults of the bank, but has not created a corresponding demand deposit entry. Thus it is excluded from the money supply and the M1 figure is reduced.

When such money, i.e. savings deposits, are added to M1 the resulting entity is called broad money supply and is denoted by M2.

B3. Reserves

The total reserves of a bank consists of the notes and coins it holds in its vaults and the amount lying to its credit at the central bank. This is what is readily available to it to support the withdrawal demands made on it — the former when cash is demanded and the latter when a cheque drawn by one of its customers is presented at another bank. Neither the origin of the notes and coins nor into which type of account they were deposited into — current, savings, time deposits or any other — makes any difference as to their standing as cash reserves.

The other types of reserves, such as Government securities and bonds, which are not as readily usable as these reserves, need not concern us here.

Terms and procedures relating to
PF stocks and shares

In this appendix we present working definitions of some terms and procedures which can be used as a basis for the development of an operational model. The main purpose here is to indicate the many issues that should be addressed in devising such a model.

The definitions of stocks and shares have not remained unchanged over time, the distinctions have become blurred, and they have acquired different meanings and connotations in different countries. For example, what was known as stocks in UK is now bonds in USA, and shares have become stocks. The stocks and shares under the PF scheme have much in common with the original British definitions of the terms, but they have also some special characteristics of their own. Therefore we have to define what we mean by PF shares and PF stocks.

C1. PF Shares

Participatory Financing Shares are ordinary shares in the "company" which consists of all the PF projects the bank is currently financing or hopes to finance in the near future. Funds obtained by selling new PF shares are to be used as venture capital for new projects. On account of the fact that every project will have a gestation period, the "company" will not be able to post a profit or loss statement on these projects until they become *operational*. Therefore PF shares cannot expect to earn a profit or loss during this period. However, since different projects will have different gestation periods and because the PF shares are not directly connected to any particular project, we have to find a way of saying when a PF share begins to earn a profit or loss. One way of doing it is for the bank to determine a common average gestation period for the projects expected to come under the PF scheme and to announce this period when the PF shares issue is advertised. The shares will not earn any profit or loss in this period of, say, one to three years. The PF shares will *mature* at the end of this gestation period. And <u>all</u> *mature* PF shares will be entitled to share in the profit/loss of <u>all</u> the *operational* projects of the "company". The "dividend" on these shares are determined on the basis of the *net* returns of all the PF projects of the bank *operational* during the bank's accounting period, say, annually.

Profit and loss accounting is done at the end of the year. Therefore the final "dividend" awarded to PF share holders is a *realised* profit/loss and not an estimated or pre-fixed one. Hence there is no room for uncertainty, speculation or *riba*. This is very important.

PF shares are transferable and have no termination points. PF shares will also have a stake in the assets of the projects. However, since the investors have no direct connection with any particular project, the claims of the PF shares are on all of the bank's PF operations. Thus, if, for example, a project ends and the assets are sold off or the bank sells off its shares in a project (perhaps to the entrepreneur or to an outside investor) the proceeds from such sales will accrue to all the PF shares (providing interim dividends, additional PF shares or increasing their value).

Whether the PF shares are issued periodically, as and when necessary or are available throughout the year, are all operational concerns and are matters for individual bank's decision. The bank may also consider issuing separate shares to different groups of projects, instead of all the investors having claims on all the projects of the bank.

C2. PF Stocks

Participatory Financing Stocks are funds deposited with the bank for a fixed period of time, to be invested in their Participatory Financing projects. The return on these investments are determined on the basis of the *net* returns of all the PF projects of the bank *operational* during the bank's accounting period, as computed at the end of that period. And the bank will use these funds mainly to advance further credits to *operational* projects. In effect, PF stocks are like fixed-term deposits except that neither the capital nor the return are guaranteed or fixed in advance.

The special characteristics of the PF stocks would be that: 1) PF stocks will not bear any fixed rate of return or interest, 2) the return will be determined at the end of each accounting period, and no attempt will be made to make any estimates in advance, 3) PF stocks are for a defined period, but it may be reinvested for another defined period, 4) PF stocks have no priority claims over PF shares, and 5) PF stocks share in profit and loss but they have no claims on the assets of the projects.

C3. PF Dividends

The "dividend" we have been talking about has one major difference as compared to other ordinary company dividends. Unlike them, the PF dividends can be positive or negative. And this is important. Its computation and disbursement are also different. Therefore we will examine them below in some detail.

C3.1 Disbursement

The *entire* net profit or loss of this "company" will be *first* distributed as "dividends" to all mature PF shares and all the stocks immediately after the announcement of accounts. No part of this net profit/loss will be held back *at this stage* for future investment or as buffer against future losses. That is, there is no retained profits or reserves at this stage. This is necessary because in the PF scheme *both* the stocks and shares participate in the profit/loss of the enterprises, unlike in the case of ordinary companies where only the share holders participate in the company's profit/loss while the stock holders' (preference shares, bonds, debentures, etc.) capital and return are guaranteed. Otherwise, if, for example, some (or all) of the profits are held back, the PF shares would rise in value at the expense of the profits of PF stocks. On the other hand, if a loss is realised and it is compensated by previously held profits, the PF stocks will escape loss at the expense of PF shares which will fall in value.

While the PF share holders and the PF stock holders will be treated equally in the computation of their "dividends" they will find themselves in different situations when it comes to the disbursement of it. If the "dividend" is positive the PF stock holder will find his capital increased, and decreased if negative. He is free to do what he will with his capital — reinvest it or take it away. On the other hand, the PF share holder may not be so free. For the Directors of the "company" may decide to retain all or part of the "dividend" due to them. If the "dividend" was positive and part of it is held back, they will receive some profit out of their investment and, at the same time, the value of their shares would rise. If negative, they would receive no profits and, in addition, their shares would fall in value.

C3.2 Computation

The net profit/loss of each PF project operational during the accounting period is obtained from its Profit and Loss account. The total net profit/loss of the "company" is obtained by summing up the profit/loss of all the individual projects. So far so good. The problem is how do we distribute the profits among the share holders and stock holders? Do the stocks and shares have equal standing? Suppose the answer is yes, then what is the relationship between a stock and a share? Are they counted in terms of units or in terms of currency? Some meaningful solution has to be found.

One way of doing it would be to first count stocks in terms of units as we do shares, and equate one unit of stock to one unit of share. Then every unit of stock will earn profit/loss the same as one unit of share. Now how do they stand in terms of currency? Is the price of a stock the same as that of a share? Which price are we talking about? The nominal value of a share, its market value or its book value? Without going into the details of why the former two are not quite suitable, let us settle down for the third — the book value of a share — and see how this can be computed and fixed in advance.

When the annual (or quarterly, half-yearly) account is made up and the "dividends" are disbursed, the shares of the "company" will have a book value as at the beginning of the next year. The price of one stock in that year can be fixed equal to this book value of one share. Thus the stocks in the "company" will be sold in integer multiples, their unit price will be the same throughout the current year (or accounting period), and every unit of stock will earn the same "dividend" as a unit of share. The price of a stock, however, may vary from year to year depending on the performance of the "company" but will be equal to the book value of the share at the beginning of the year and will remain the same throughout that year.

Consequently, as far as the computation of "dividend" is concerned, the company has a total of this many units of "shares" and the "dividend" per unit is obtained by dividing the total net profit/loss of the "company" by this number of "shares". This "dividend" per unit is then the same for PF shares as well as for PF stocks.

C4. PF Projects and the PF "Company"

Now we have to explain what we mean by projects and the "company" in the foregoing paragraphs, in the context of participatory financing. Each PF Project is an independent business entity whose legal status in the eyes of the Company Law may be a private limited liability company. The project can be anything from a large manufacturing concern to a small medical laboratory. There are two main and essential partners in each project: the participate-financing bank and the concerned entrepreneur. The entrepreneur is the active partner and the bank is the "sleeping" partner.

In distributing the profit/loss of the project, the profit/loss accruing to both the bank and the investor will be, in the first instance, credited to the bank. The bank will collect all such profit/loss from all its projects and then divide it between itself and its investors.

This collection and distribution as well as all other matters to and fro between the projects and the bank will be handled by this umbrella organisation we have called the "company", which can be a separate unit within the bank or even a subsidiary.

List of Variables in Appendix A

KI$	Capital invested by the investor (in dollars)
CM	Credit multiplying factor used by the bank
KB$	Capital invested by the bank (in dollars)
PP$	Profit achieved by the project (in dollars)
SB	Share of the bank in the profit
SE	Share of the entrepreneur in the profit
SI	Share of the investor in the profit
PB$	Profit due to the bank (in dollars)
PE$	Profit due to the entrepreneur (in dollars)
PI$	Profit due to the investor (in dollars)
PP	Profit rate achieved by the project
PI	Profit rate realised by the investor
INF	Rate of inflation
PPN$	Profit achieved by the project after compensating the investor for the loss of his capital due to inflation (in dollars)
PPN	Profit rate of the project after the compensation
PIN$	Profit realised by the investor after compensating for the loss suffered by his capital due to inflation (in dollars)
PIN	Profit rate of the investor after the compensation
PP'	Threshold point
PPN'	Threshold point when profit is calculated net of inflation
SBL	Share of the bank in loss
SIL	Share of the investor in loss

Bibliography

1. Ahmad, Khurshid (ed.), *Studies in Islamic Economics*. Leicester: Islamic Foundation, (1980).
2. ---------------, Elimination of *riba*: concept and problems. In: Institute of Policy Studies, 1994. pp.33-63.
3. Gafoor, A.L.M. Abdul, *Interest-free Commercial Banking*. Groningen: Apptec Publications, 1995.
4. Hutchinson, H.D., *Money, Banking and the U.S. Economy*. 7th ed. Englewood Cliffs, NJ: Prentice Hall, 1992.
5. Iqbal, Zubair and Abbas Mirakhor, *Islamic Banking*. Washington, DC: International Monetary Fund, Occasional Paper No.49, 1987.
6. Institute of Policy Studies, *Elimination of Riba from the Economy*. Islamabad: IPS, 1994.
7. King, David, *Banking & Money*. London: Edward Arnold, 1987.
8. Korteweg, S. and F.A.G. Keesing, *A Textbook of Money*. London: Longmans, 1959.
9. Pemberton, Sir Leigh (the Governor of the Bank of England) From a speech given to the Arab Bankers' Association. *Meed*, 5 October 1984, p.2. Quoted in: Rad (1991).
10. Qadir, Ghulam, Interest-free banking: a proposal. In: Institute of Policy Studies, 1994. pp.105-116.
11. Rad, Tourani A., *Theoretical and practical aspects of the interest-free banking system*. Amsterdam: Nederlands Institut voor het Bank- en Effectenbedrijf, 1991.
12. Robertson, H., *Money*. Cambridge Economic Handbooks II. London: Nisbet & Co. 1937.
13. Saleh, Nabil A., *Unlawful gain and legitimate profit in Islamic law: Riba, gharar and Islamic Banking*. Cambridge: Cambridge University Press, 1986.
14. Schotta, C., Unresolved Issues for the Islamic Baking Operations in the United States, *Arabia*, February 1985, pp.64-65. Quoted in: Rad (1991).

15.Siddiqi, Muhammad Nejatullah, *Banking Without Interest.* Leicester: The Islamic Foundation, 1988.

16.Steele, F., Islamic Banks Operating in the Western Countries. Paper presented at the *Conference on Islamic Banking: Its impact on world financial and commercial practices*, London, 18 September 1984. Quoted in: Rad (1991).

17.Suratgar, D., Prospects for co-operation between Western and Islamic Financial Systems. Paper presented at the *Conference on Islamic Banking: Its impact on the world financial and commercial practices*, London, 18 September 1984. pp.28-34. Quoted in: Rad (1991).

18.Withers, H., *The Meaning of Money.* 3rd ed. London: John Murray, 1923.

19.Zaman, S.M. Hasanuz-, Practical options for Central and Commercial banking. In: Institute of Policy Studies, 1994. pp.197-216.

Index